Buckfastleigh:
A Town in the Making

Sandra Coleman

Bridge Street, Buckfastleigh   28094

This version of the book is virtually as originally published, presenting the work of Sandra Coleman. There are now additional pages at the back providing information about the publisher, Arthur L Clamp.

The republishing project is being managed by Arthur's grandson, Steven Gibson. We aim to find all the research that he was involved in publishing, preserving it for the next generation as part of 'The Clamp Collection'.

INTRODUCTION

IN THIS book, which has been written for local people, I have attempted to trace the development of Buckfastleigh through the ages. Alan Rogers, in his book, *This was Their World*, wrote that, "A historian is either concerned with the *place* that he is studying or with the *people* who formerly lived there." As I confess to the second concern this short book is primarily about past Buckfastleigh families and individuals and the contribution they made to the industrial and social development of our town. The descriptions of Buckfastleigh as it was in the early part of this century are seen through the eyes of present day inhabitants who were born and brought up in the town and their stories about the Buckfastleigh of their childhood I have found most interesting.

Not all those who came to regard Buckfastleigh as their home were born in the town, of course. In fact, from early times invasion and exile have brought immigrants from France, Germany and Poland. Our French origins are particularly strong which might make for some unease among those who consider the French very foreign with ways quite alien to the more down to earth Devonian!

The research for this book has been fascinating and I have come to know better many local people I have known since childhood days, teachers, shopkeepers and neighbours and whose local knowledge, support and keen interest gave me the stimulus I needed to complete this book.

Because of the vastness of the subject there are aspects of life I have not touched upon or have mentioned only briefly. I have concentrated on people whose life in days gone by—and not so long ago either—was often hard; and yet there was a kind of pioneering spirit which sustained them.

It is for the descendants of these people and for those who live in Buckfastleigh today that this book is written. Other than in tourist manuals—and then only because of the situation of Buckfast Abbey—Buckfastleigh is rarely mentioned in books or articles. Yet a sense of history pervades the town and it is this heritage which should keep us together in these days when community life and the identity of many small towns and villages is fast disappearing.

Sandra Coleman,
13 Chapel Street,
Buckfastleigh,
South Devon,
June, 1982.

Sandra Coleman, born and brought up in Buckfastleigh, was educated first at Buckfastleigh Primary School and then Totnes High School for Girls. She has worked for many years as a youth and community worker since qualifying at Westhill College, Selly Oak, Birmingham, and has lived in Greece and Australia. At the present time she is working in London.

Although not her first venture into writing, this is her first book and clearly shows her feelings and appreciation of her birthplace in spite of spending many years away from it. This may, however, have given her more perspective on the town and will, it is hoped, encourage readers to adopt a similar perspective to the places in which they have grown up.

Chapter One
EARLY HISTORY

IN THOSE dark days well before Christ was born, Britain was invaded by many different tribes of people. From about 500 BC onwards the Celts inhabited Britain with those living in the north called *Gaels* and those living in the south called *Britons*. It is commonly believed that these people were peasant farmers who had come to Britain from across the Channel and who lived in tribes and clans.

Farming Dartmoor and the land around it must have been hard and unrewarding. The primitive shelters they built could not have been much protection against the weather and the wild animals. We know from excavations in Buckfastleigh caves that animals such as wolves, wild cats, hyenas and bears roamed wild (and further back in time rhinoceros, elephants and cave lions).

Life probably continued in much the same way for hundreds of years. Traders came from across the Channel, pirates and other invaders, too. Julius Caesar first invaded Britain in 54 BC although the actual conquest of the country did not take place until nearly a hundred years later.

The celtic kingdom of the Dumonii—Cornwall, Devon and western Somerset—saw a fairly peaceful period under the Romans. Then, in 400 AD the Roman soldiers were called back to defend Rome against the attacks of the Goths, leaving Britain wide open for the next invaders of Britain, the Anglo Saxons who made regular attacks from 449 AD onwards. Finally, after many years the Saxons drove the Britons to Cornwall, Wales and Brittany almost bringing to an end the ancient kingdom of the Dumonii in England.

The Saxons founded kingdoms of their own naming them Wessex, Sussex, Essex, Middlesex and Mercia. The Angles founded the eastern kingdom of Northumbria and East Anglia finally giving their name to the land which they had conquered calling it *Angleland*.

The Anglo Saxons settled down to farming the country and lived in farms protected by a stockade and a moat. Those of the original Britons who were left were pushed out to less fertile parts of Devon whilst the Saxons took over the more fertile land.

Life continued to be hard with warfare between the tribes, plagues and the hard, hard winters to contend with. The most notable event of the period—which changed the life of the whole country—was the arrival of St. Augustine in 597 AD. The invasion of the country by the Anglo Saxons, and the gradual conversion of the tribes to Christianity, is told by the Venerable Bede (673 to 735) in the first English history book ever written.

So life continued for another two hundred years until the Danes arrived on the scene and made repeated attacks on Britain. They became bolder as the years went by until the attacks came as far west as Devon. This was the period when Alfred became king of Wessex from 871 AD and engaged in frequent battles with the Danes until in 878 peace was made and the Danish King Guthrain was baptised as a Christian.

After brief raids in 893 there was no more trouble for ninety years, a lifetime of peace for some people, and then the Danes renewed their attacks on England. The King (for by this time there was a king of all England) massacred Danes living in England and the invading Danes made a great attack. Ethelred, the king, fled to France and finally the Danish King, Canute, added England to his Scandinavian empire reigning from 1016 to 1035 AD.

Although life changed far more slowly than it does today, a great many changes had taken place from when the Romans left Britain to the arrival of King Canute. Life was more ordered, more established. There were no more scattered tribes fighting each other indiscriminately. The country was divided into regions each with a king who ruled, the stronger one being the one who ruled the whole country.

With the coming of King Canute we have our first introduction to Buckfast Abbey in *Buckfaesten* as it was then known. The late Dom John Stephan, of Buckfast Abbey, wrote a most interesting and comprehensive book on the origins and history of Buckfast Abbey, so it is only necessary to say that Canute, who not only gave England stability but many years of peace in which to develop, became a staunch supporter of the Christian tradition. After intensive investigation Dom John Stephan firmly believed that it was through Canute and one of his English thegns that Buckfast Abbey was founded in approximately 1018.

"The first monks of Buckfast most probably came from either Tavistock or Winchester". According to Dom John's investigation both monasteries were well thought of by Canute who also had a great liking for the Abbot Lyfing of Tavistock. The rule of life in the monasteries was based on the rule of St. Benedict, the Divine Office, manual labour and study.

Canute was succeeded in turn by his two sons and, on the death of his second son, the Witan invited Edward the Confessor, the son of the last Saxon king, to take the crown. After reigning for twenty years he died without an heir and his cousin, William of Normandy, claimed the crown. However, the Witan had already invited Harold, the late king's brother-in-law to be king and thus the scene was set for the Battle of Hastings in 1066.

Harold was killed, as we know, but it was not for some years after that William could claim to have conquered all England. Up and down the country there were uprisings and battles from resistance groups and interference from other countries. Eventually William succeeded but before initiating change he wanted to know exactly what England and the Barons had to offer in the way of land, gold, houses and resources generally. So, in 1086, Commissioners were sent from county to county to acquire information and the results of their survey are recorded in the Domesday Book.

The Domesday Book is a fascinating book to read. Reference libraries have copies of the county histories and the compilers of the Victoria County History of Devonshire have translated and pieced together the information contained in the Domesday Book which includes the Exeter Book. What an undertaking in those days when there was no fast transport and no effective way of communicating to facilitate the collation of information.

The returns for the counties of Devonshire, Cornwall and Somerset were with the Bishop of Exeter where, no doubt, the Exeter book was compiled. Three entries are of particular interest to Buckfast and Buckfastleigh people for we see reference, if not to Buckfastleigh itself, to Buckfast and areas surrounding it. First of all, the book describes lands that the Abbot of Buckfast held:

LAND OF THE ABBOT OF BULFESTRA CHURCH IN DEVONESCIRA....

The Abbot has a manor called Bulfestra and it is the seat (caput) of the Abbey and never paid geld. There the Abbot has 1 smith and 10 serfs who have 2 ploughs; there the Abbot has 3 swine and wood (land) 1 league in length by ½ league in width.

What of a man called William de Falesia? The Domesday Book describes the lands held by this man who was not a Buckfastleigh person, of that I am sure, but one who would have had considerable influence in the area:

William has a manor called DENA (Dean) which William called TRE and it paid geld for 3 hides. These 12 ploughs can till. Four knights hold it of William. Thereof the knights have 1 hide and 3 ploughs in demesne and the villeins 2 hides and 6 ploughs. There the knights have 19 villeins, 15 borders, 2 serfs, 16 beasts, 13 swine, 70 sheep, 50 goats, 6 acres of wood(land), 10 acres of meadow a 1 league of pasture worth 4 pound when William received it the same.

Of the aforesaid manor a certain Englishman holds land enough whence to pay William 10 shillings a year. He held it TRE but could not be independent of his lord.

Note the term, *Englishman*. It suggests that the land was mostly in the hands of French overlords, this *Englishman* being a notable exception.

William de Falesia certainly did well out of King William's conquest of England, as it says in the Victoria County History of Devon:

To William de Falesia's share fell, when the spoils of the conquest were divided, 19 manors within the county of Devon assessed at 16½ hides and comprising some twelve thousand acres under cultivation.

Of these manors... Holne, Dean, Rattery and Dartington have been the Saxon Alwin's.

William de Falesia must certainly have been a well known man locally.

What was his day like? Society now was well ordered, that is each man, woman and child had his or her place in life clearly defined. The feudal system had begun with a vengeance. The head of the estate was the Lord of the manor and he lived in his demesne which was the Lord's home farm. The remainder of his land was occupied by villagers many of whom were his dependants. They lived there on condition that they cultivated the land for him.

One wonders what the effect must have been on the local people who had to succumb yet again to invaders, and invaders who had come to stay. However, there had been no mass killings or enslavement so that the ordinary person probably found his daily life little changed. It was probably the wealthier families who had land and property taken away and given to the Normans who were hardest hit.

Several well known Buckfastleigh families came to Britain from France. The Furneaux family, for instance, most probably originated from a man who came over with William the Conqueror. It is also recorded that King Henry II appointed a *Galfride de Furnel* or *Furneaus* to be the first annual Sherriff of Devon in 1154. We hear more of the early Furneaux in connection with other places in Devon. The Buckfastleigh connection is not evident until about the seventeenth century.

Another well known family were the Hamlyns, also, it is believed, descended from the Normans. They apparently came to Devon and Cornwall in the train of the Earl of Cornwall, Robert of Montaigne. Robert of Montaigne was the half brother of William the Conqueror who held twenty-two manors in Cornwall for which the Hamlyns were responsible.

Of the Cabell family it was Walter Cabell who came to England at about the time of the Conquest and settled in Wiltshire. His family and descendants spread themselves around the counties of Wiltshire, Dorset, Somerset and Devon, the Devonian family settling in Buckfastleigh.

Chapter Two
MEDIAEVAL LIFE AND THE RISE AND FALL OF BUCKFAST ABBEY

BUCKFAST ABBEY went through considerable change when Stephen came to the throne in 1136. Because he wanted "an infusion of new blood", as Dom John Stephan puts it, Buckfast came under the domination of the house of Savigny in France, on the special request of King Stephen, with the result that many French monks and a French Abbot came to Buckfast. However, within twelve years, due to monastic reform which spread all over Europe, Buckfast became a Cistercian Order.

Under the reign of King John, who followed Stephen, much of the lands and possessions of Buckfast were confiscated by the king. However, during the thirteenth century the wool industry flourished in England. The Cistercians led its development in several counties and, according to Dom John Stephan, not least in Buckfast as the Cistercians found accessible ports in Exeter, Teignmouth, Dartmouth and Kingsbridge for exporting their wool. The free grazing on Dartmoor was a boon to the Abbot of Buckfast and lay landowners who were active economically and socially. The monks, held in high esteem, received many donations and grants. This was certainly an interesting period which Dom John Stephan describes in detail in his book, *Buckfast Abbey, A Short History and Guide*.

We know that in this period when Buckfast was a thriving wool centre Buckfastleigh was an "overspill town" of Buckfast, as some people have described it, with people engaged in spinning and weaving in their homes.

Buckfastleigh is well situated. It is sheltered and surrounded by rich farm land and well served with brooks and leats. These geographical advantages must have had considerable bearing in the development of Buckfastleigh as an industrial centre. Not only has it been a centre for the woollen industry, but as Helen Harris, the authoress, records in her book, *Industrial Archeology of Dartmoor* . . . "there were a number of copper mines around Buckfastleigh and Ashburton. Chief of these was Brookfield situated about two miles north-west of Buckfastleigh (in the grounds of Brook Manor)." Apparently, there are also extensive remains of early tinning operations on Buckfastleigh Moor and around the source of Wella Brook and the Mardle.

One of the first recorded entries made about Buckfastleigh came on the death of Abbot William Gifford in 1349. Philip was elected Abbot in his place on 21st May, 1349, and in the following year he obtained a grant to his Abbey of a weekly market to Buckfastleigh, on Tuesdays, and a yearly fair at Brent. How long the Buckfastleigh market continued I don't know but an unsuccessful attempt to revive it was made early in the twentieth century.

Mr Leslie Lane propping up an important find — the old market board giving details of tolls to be paid. *Courtesy of Mr. L. Lane.*

By the fourteenth century Holy Trinity Parish Church was well established in Buckfastleigh. As it is a landmark for miles around it is safe to assume that it was a landmark to the people of mediaeval Buckfastleigh. The original church was probably built in the twelfth century (according to a plaque in the church porch the first vicar took up his living in 1263) and was of a simple rectangular plan to which, late in the thirteenth century, a tower and transepts were added to produce a cruciform plan.

Buckfastleigh churchyard as seen from the tower.

One wonders why it was built so far out of town. Our late vicar, Rev. John Timms, thought that it was more likely that when the settlement of Buckfastleigh first started to develop it was in the vicinity of the church; but, that, as the woollen industry thrived the population began to settle down the hill near to the water power.

Although life was fine for the French nobles in their big houses, life for the ordinary families during the Middle Ages was raw and hard. Rural areas in particular provided only a mean living for the men who farmed the land and battled against the elements. But, in both town and country, plagues wasted the population and dirty, cramped and unhygienic conditions in the home and in the streets ensured that disease was never very far away.

In England unemployment was rife and country people flocked to the towns and cities to find work many of them becoming vagrants. However, with the wool trade flourishing in Buckfast there was work available which provided income for some local people.

It was a colourful and tempestuous period commencing with the Hundred Years War with France in 1338 and the Black Death plague taking its toll of human lives in Europe from 1348 and spreading to England in the following year; Kings deposed one another and England laid claim to the throne of France; Joan of Arc saved the French town of Orleans only to be burnt at the stake in 1431; uprisings in England and the beginnings of the Wars of the Roses in 1455. One wonders how the lives of ordinary men and women were affected by these events. Certainly the plague was no respecter of persons and if rural people managed to evade politics it was certain that they could not avoid the plague which took thousands of lives all over Europe and which must have affected Buckfastleigh, too.

Henry VIII came to the throne in 1509. His reign saw the birth of the Reformation. The religious changes which he made in his lifetime affected the ordinary people in no uncertain way. Of all the changes in the next fifty years the change which affected local people most was the Dissolution of the Monasteries in 1536 by King Henry aided by Thomas Cromwell.

Dom John Stephan, in his book on Buckfast Abbey, describes how, after the death of Abbot Rede in 1535, a "new Abbot was appointed not chosen by the monks but intruded by Thomas Cromwell who was thus enabled to reward one of his devoted servants", it seems that the way for an easy conquest by Henry VIII was being prepared. An Abbot who was favourable to the king and Cromwell would offer little resistance. The new Abbot's name was Gabriel Donne . . . *a Cistercian monk of Straford, Westham.*

King Henry had for many years been fighting the authority of the Pope especially in the matter of his divorces. In 1536 an Act of Parliament supressed those religious houses which did not have a revenue of £200 a year. The deed of surrender was signed in 1539 and through the acquiessance of the Abbot, Gabriel Donne, it was an easy surrender. Buckfast Abbey was stripped and laid bare of all its possessions; the lead from the roof was sold, the money going to the crown; and the Abbey's bells were bought by the people of Buckfastleigh for the parish church. The buildings, church and lands were given to Sir Thomas Denys and remained in his family until the eighteenth century.

Holy Trinity church bells after being recast and ready to be rehung sometime during the 1920s. John Warren, warden, is in the background. *Courtesy of Mrs. E. Walters.*

The Deed of Surrender signed by the Abbot was witnessed by nine monks. No doubt they were rewarded in some way for the part they played. What happened to the men who remained faithful to the church we do not know. Throughout England this same wanton destruction was repeated. In Buckfast and Buckfastleigh it was a closure which affected everybody both spiritually and economically.

It was the Dissolution of the Priory of Plympton which made the Manor of Dean available for purchase again. Henry II had given the manor into the keeping of the Priory, together with Dean Church, until the Dissolution when it was returned to the crown.

A man called William Giles of Bowden bought the manor from the crown and John Giles, his son, built Dean Court late in the sixteenth century. William's grandson, Edward Giles, born at Totnes in 1556, inherited the Manor of Dean to which he eventually retired. When he died in 1637 he was buried in the south aisle of the parish church at Dean. Eventually it came into the hands of the Yarde family until 1789, *when the heiress of Yarde married Frances Buller, Justice of the Court of the King's Bench, who was created a baronet in the same year. His descendant, Sir John Yarde Buller, was called to the House of Lords in 1858 under the title of Baron Churston.*

Chapter Three

THE CABELLS AND THE CIVIL WAR

DESCENDED from the Normans, as mentioned previously, branches of the Cabell family were scattered all over the West Country. The first mention of a Buckfastleigh connection was of Richard Cabell, the son of Richard Cabell of Frome in Somerset, who lived at Brook Manor and married Susannah Peter, daughter of John Peter of Buckfastleigh, sometime prior to 1581.

Susannah was related to the famous Sir William Petre, Secretary of State under Henry VIII, Edward VI and Elizabeth. He was a Devon man and yielded a great deal of influence due to the powerful position he held and the shrewdness of his character. According to one historian he achieved financial gain from the dissolution of the monasteries. Richard and Susannah Cabell had two sons, Richard and Samuel, and two daughters. This Richard, born in 1582, was the father of the infamous Richard Cabell who was hated so much by local people.

Richard and Samuel were considered gentlemen and were probably highly respected among local people. Certainly we know that they were churchwardens at the Parish Church and that their lives, as all others at this time, were affected by the Civil Wars.

It was King Charles I who plunged England into a Civil War, a war that was to divide the whole country and turn neighbour against neighbour and county against county. Kind Charles was often in conflict with the Parliament of the day and thought that he could dismiss it whenever he wanted. The final clash came in 1629 over the levying of duties on imports and exports and innovations in religion. Parliament could stand no more and, led by Oliver Cromwell, was determined to rid the country of the king who seemed bent on bringing ruin to Britain.

It seemed that Devon, on the whole, favoured Sir Oliver Cromwell, but historians take pains to point out that not all Devonians favoured Parliament, there were many more who still favoured the king.

In all the accounts of the battles which were fought in Devon it appears that the armies' routes bypassed Buckfastleigh. "Ashburton and district" are frequently mentioned and whether Buckfastleigh is included in "the district" it is difficult to say.

Maurice Ashley, in his book, *The English Civil Wars*, says, quote: "What of the common people? They suffered most in parts of the country which were overcome by soldiers requiring food, horses and "free quarter", which was not at once paid for. On the other hand, the demands of war created full employment and increased the earnings of labour. Some ordinary men were glad to enlist in an army or navy to secure a share of the plunder . . ."

E. A. Andriette, in his book, *Devon and Exeter in the Civil Wars*, indicates that: "Certain communities and individuals had long since made up their mind as to which side they would support. The corporation of Plymouth, Barnstaple, Dartmouth and Exeter had given repeated assurances to Parliament of their loyal support . . . smaller communities such as Totnes, Tiverton and Axminster were much more circumspect."

In 1641, between the first and second Civil Wars, Parliament executed Thomas Wentworth, Earl of Strafford, as a traitor. He had been one of the King's principal advisers and was feared by Parliament. Before his execution there had been an unsuccessful attempt by King Charles to rescue Strafford from the Tower of London which had caused rioting.

Parliament declared that it was necessary to ensure that the King had good counsellors to advise him and ten members of Parliament were selected to draw up a form of protestation. The Protestation agreed upon in parliament was signed by the protestant peers who had to profess that *I . . . do, in the presence of Almighty God promise, vow and protest to maintain and defend . . . the true reformed Protestant religion.*

On 6th May, 1641, a bill was introduced in the House of Commons imposing the signing of the Protestation on all Englishmen over eighteen years of age. It suggested that those who refused to sign were not eligible to hold office. A letter of instruction was sent out to all the Sheriffs and Justices of the Peace who were obliged to take the oath themselves. Then, after various local officials had attested before the J.P.s the parish priest read out the Protestation in the church on the Sunday and the people signed it in front of him and the officials.

BUCKFASTLEIGH PARISH

Devon Protestation Returns for 1641 giving the names of 330 local inhabitants of that time. See how familiar the names are.

Adames, Stephen	Bovey, Nathaniel	Cater, John	Cropping, Thomas
Adams, Peter	Bovey, Robert sen.	Chafe, Richard sen.	Cropping, Thomas
Alegood, John	Bovey, Robert jun.	Chasse, James	Cropping, William
Alegood, William	Bovey, Thomas	Chasse, John	Crusse, Obidiah
Anselow, John	Bovey, Thomas	Chasse, John	Culme, William
Austyne, Alfred	Bovey, William	Chasse, Matthew	Cuttiwen, John
Austyne, Alfred	Bownsall, Andrew	Chasse, Richard jun.	Dal, James
Austyne, David	Brodford, John	Chasse, Thomas	Davey, Walter
Austyne, John	Brooking, Walter	Chasse, William	Day, Hugh
Austyne, Thomas	Brown, Jezrael	Chasten, Thomas	Derry, Michael
Austyne, Thomas	Browne, Robert	Coffe, Roger	Derry, Richard
Ball, John	Browne, William	Collings, John	Dod, John
Ball, William	Browse, Martin	Collings, William	Dod, John
Bartley, Andrew	Browse, Richard	Combe, William	Dod, Samuel
Bartley, David	Buckinham, Robert	Cooke, Daniel	Dodridge, Francis
Bartley, Stephen	Burgis, Thomas	Cooke, David	Dolbert, Robert
Beard, Andrew	Buttaven, Richard	Cooke, John	Downeing, Richard
Beard, Anthony	Buttaver, Joseph	Cooke, John	Dunscombe, Thomas
Beard, Edmund	Cabell, Richard jun.	Cooke, Nicholas	Edmund, Thomas
Benuet, Peter	Cabell, Samuel	Cooke, Thomas	Edmunds, John sen.
Bickam, Ellis	Callard, Samuel	Cooke, Thomas	Edmunds, John jun.
Bicott, George	Callerd, Abraham	Couch, George	Edwards, Matthew
Binmoore, Henry	Callerd, Charles sen.	Couch, William	Eles, Thomas
Binmoore, Robert	Callerd, Henry	Crapping, Robert	Elles, Thomas
Bovey, Christopher	Callerd, John	Creppin, Simon	Emmott, George
Bovey, Evan	Callerd, Thomas jun.	Crimpe, Peter	Evines, John
Bovey, John	Case, William	Cropping, John	Fabian, George
Bovey, John	Casey, Christopher	Cropping, Michael	Fogwell, Thomas

Fogwell, William sen.	Huniwell, Jonas	Parnell, Benjamin	Stone, John sen.
Fogwell, William	Ilbert, William	Parnell, John	Stoneing, Richard
Ford, Thomas	Jacson, Nicholas	Pernell, Benjamin	Stowe, John
Forster, Philip	Jellerd, Richard	Perry, Robert	Sumper, James
Foster, Richard	Jewell, Edmund	Pethabridge, Edward	Symons, Philip
Foxe, James	Jewell, Giles	Pethabridge, Emmanuel	Tapper, Richard
Foxe, Samuel	Kelland, Samuel	Pethabridge, John	Taylor, Jarvis
Foxe, Thomas	Kelland, Thomas	Pethabridge, Nicholas	Toope, David
Foxe, William	Knapman, John	Pethabridge, Nicholas	Toope, John
Foxworthy, John	Knapman, Thomas	Pethabridge, Thomas	Toope, John
Frye, John	Kyttow, Edmund	Phylip, Andrew	Toope, Samuel
Fryer, John	Lang, John	Phylipp, Christopher	Toope, Thomas
Fynch, William	Lang, John	Phylipp, Jonathan	Toope, Thomas
Gatchfeeld, John	Lange, Samuel	Phylipp, William	Toope, William
Gee, John	Langly, David	Phylips, Christopher	Torre, Edward
Gray, Charles	Langston, Samuel	Pittiven, Edward	Torre, James
Gray, John	Langworthy, Owen	Pomery, Elias	Torre, Peter
Gray, John jun.	Lavers, Martin	Pomery, James	Treeby, Elias
Gray, John jun.	Lavers, William	Pope, Andrew	Tucker, Daniel
Greene, Edward	Luscombe, Philip	Poundey, Edmund	Tucker, John
Grose, Bartholomew	Luscombe, Samuel jun.	Prouse, William	Turgis, Jasper
Grose, John	Maddocke, Henry	Putteven, Peter	Turgis, John
Grose, John jun.	Maddocke, Henry	Putteven, William	Turgis, Thomas
Gydley, Hercules	Maddocke, Samuel	Putteven, William	Turgis, Thomas
Gydley, John	Man, Austin	Puttiven, James	Turner, Walter
Gydley, Thomas	Man, Richard	Puttiven, Philip	Tuscombe, Samuel
Hall, Ezekiel	Man, Thomas	Rees, Walter	Tymkam, Andrew
Hall, George	Marrocke, Richard	Remell, Anthony	Tynckam, Robert
Hanaford, John	Mitchelmore, John	Rendell, Edward	Veale, William
Hanaford, Philip	Mitchelmore, John	Robins, Walter	Voysey, John
Hanaford, Thomas	Mitchelmore, John	Rovers, Henry	Warring, John
Hanniford, Andrew	Mitchelmore, Peter	Sandey, Henry sen.	Wartley, Edmund
Harford, John	Mitchelmore, Robert	Sandey, Henry jun.	Waysey, Edward
Harris, Edmund	Mitchelmore, Walter	Sandey, Jonas	Weeger, Thomas
Harris, John	Mitchelmore, William	Sandey, Laurence	Westlake, Samuel
Harris, John	Morgan, James	Sarle, George	Whyte, John
Harris, John	Moore, William	Satchfeeld, Charles	Williams, Edward
Harvey, John	Mudge, Bartholomew	Satchfeeld, Charles	Wills, Roger
Harwell, John jun.	Mudge, George	Scorce, Henry	Windyet, John
Hill, Nathaniel	Mudge, John	Shaper, Edward jun.	Windyet, John
Hodge, John	Mudge, Nicholas	Shaper, John	Withecombe, Henry
Hodge, Robert	Mudge, Thomas	Shaper, Roger	Withecombe, Thomas
Hodge, Thomas	Mudge, Thomas	Shapter, Nicholas	Withecombe, William
Hore, Nicholas	Mudge, William	Sharpham, Laurence	Wolson, Thomas
Hore, Nicholas	Nicholls, Simon	Sheere, Richard	Woode, Peter
Hore, Robert	Noleworthy, Robert jun.	Shellabeer, Walter	Wotton, Geoffrey
Hore, William	Norraway, John	Sherwell, Hugh	Wotton John
Hore, William	Norris, Henry	Sherwell, John sen.	Wotton, Richard
Horwell, Richard	Northway, Christopher	Sherwell, John jun.	Wotton, William
Howell, William	Northway, William	Sherwell, John	Wrepford, Henry
Huniwell, George	Noseworthy, Robert	Sherwell, Peter	
Huniwell, John	Oxford, Thomas	Steevens, Samuel	
Huniwell, John	Oxford, William	Stonding, John	
Huniwell, John	Page, Nicholas	Stone, John	

(The above names in the same hand, the following seven are signatures.)

John Dolbeare   Vicar
Henry Luscombe + Constable
Philip Furnape   Constable
John Warringe   Churchwarden
John Bovey   Churchwarden
John Shapter + Overseer
John Stone + Overseer

However, as a guide to the population of Buckfastleigh at that time it is of limited value. For a start, with the exception of a couple of Cornish parishes, no women were expected to sign and no one under eighteen years of age. Neither was it signed by Roman Catholics of course. It does not appear that Roman Catholics were actually punished or mistreated for failing to sign the Protestation but it meant that they were effectively barred from taking any public office.

Ordinary people had very little concern for the wars and the arguments between the King and Parliament and only wanted to be left alone to carry on their daily life. But the years 1642 to 1646 were disastrous for Devon which was invaded and crossed by armies time and time again.

In an April edition of the Western Morning News in 1932 an article appeared concerning the find of mediaeval coins unearthed during excavation work in Buckfastleigh. The article said that the exact location was not known but the coroner suggested that the coins were probably a Civil War hoard. Apparently, Oliver Cromwell's brother, Richard, owned a considerable amount of land in the neighbourhood of Buckfastleigh and he had come across a deed bearing his signature regarding land not far from Ashburton. The coins were:

        One James I shilling.
        One James I sixpence.
        Two Charles I shillings.
        Two Charles I sixpences.
        Three Philip IV coins.
        Five Elizabethan shillings.
        Eight Elizabethan sixpences.

Not a great deal of wealth by today's standards, but to someone of that day an unexpected windfall culled from some plunder.

Richard Cabell died in 1653, in the year that Cromwell declared himself Lord Protector of England, and was succeeded by his son, the infamous Richard Cabell who was the last of the Cabells in this locally well known line. This Richard married Elizabeth Fowell of Ugborough in January 1654 to 1655. They had only one daughter who, on her marriage, carried the line and the estate into the family of Fownes.

What it was that he actually did to earn such an evil reputation as he had locally is not easily apparent. It has been suggested that it might have had its origins in a law suit brought by Cabell against William Ellacott and others regarding the use of the Town Mills in Buckfastleigh and Kilbury Mills which Ellacott rented.

Richard Cabell was so hated and feared, however, that when he died in approximately 1677 his tomb was encased by a mausoleum to prevent his escape! He was immortalised by Sir Arthur Conan Doyle, the author, who based his book, *The Hounds of the Baskervilles*, on the legendary "hounds of hell" which, it was believed, chased Sir Richard when he escaped from his tomb on the night of his death and galloped off on his horse down the drive of Brook Manor!

His death was not recorded in the parish register, although the death of his wife in 1686 is recorded in rather an ominous manner. The register says that,

Mrs. Elizabeth Cabell was buried in Linnen and the penalty for transgression satisfyeth as appeareth in a certificate from Sir William Bastard.

Thus ended the Cabells as Lords of the Manor of Buckfastleigh. Yet from that day to this local children have had passed down to them the solemn warning that if they walk around Richard Cabell's mausoleum seven times and put their fingers through the bars they will be bitten off!

William Cabell, the last Richard's brother, left Buckfastleigh for Warminster in 1664. William's son, Nicholas, married Rachel Hooper of Frome in the St. John the Baptist Church there and it was their son, William, who went to America in approximately 1726. That really is another story but it is thanks to the descendants of William Cabell in the United States that we know so much of the history of the Cabell family.

Descendants of Dr. William Cabell are now spread all over the United States. In fact, there are about 250 members of the Cabell Foundation which meet annually at some place which is connected with the Cabells, usually in Virginia, and with an average attendance of one hundred.

The American branch of the family have been prominent in all works of life, in the church, in politics, medicine, military life and society. In the spring of 1979 a group of about ten people, members of the Cabell Foundation Inc. came to Buckfastleigh whilst on a ten day visit to England. The group was led by genealogist and past President of the Foundation, Mrs. J. Ferneyhough, who told me that the group were visiting areas where their ancestors had once lived, including Buckfastleigh, Frome and Warminster. Since their visit Mrs. Ferneyhough has been instrumental in donating to the people of Buckfastleigh, a book, written and published in 1895 about the descendants of William Cabell, called, *The Cabells and Their Kin*.

ROBERT HERRICK

One famous Royalist, of whom we must make mention before this chapter ends, was Robert Herrick who reluctantly left his London life and friends to become the vicar of Dean Prior in 1629. He had a love hate relationship with Devon and her people and in 1647 when he was dismissed from his living because of his Royalist sympathies he wrote this farewell poem:

> *Dean Bourne, farewell; I never look to see*
> *Deane, or thy warty incivility.*
> *A people currish; churlish as the seas;*
> *and rude (almost) as rudest Savages.*
> *With whom I did, and may re-sojourne when*
> *Rockes turn to rivers, rivers turn to men.*

However, after the Restoration Herrick returned to Dean Prior where he remained vicar until his death in 1674 at the age of eighty-four years.

Part Two
THE DEVELOPMENT OF BUCKFASTLEIGH

Chapter Four
THE HAMLYNS

Joseph Hamlyn, 1807–1888   John Hamlyn, 1816–1878   William Hamyln, 1852– .

WITH THE dissolution of Buckfast Abbey in 1539 the woollen trade did not die out but continued with families spinning and weaving in their homes. In her book, *Industrial Archeology of Dartmoor* Helen Harris records that in 1838 there were 700 looms in Buckfastleigh more than in any other town in the country and a quarter of all the remaining ones in Devon.

The structure of Buckfastleigh, as I have already said, bears witness to the past for the town is well served with rivers and leats and the ope ways of the town, Dials Court, Warren's Court and Moore's Court lead to the rivers where the wool was washed. With the development of the woollen industry, that is from hand loom to machinery, Buckfastleigh really came into its own as a centre for wool and mainly through the Hamlyn family who had such an impact on the life and development of the town in the nineteenth century.

They were from the beginning large landowners and, Joseph Hamlyn senior, in the early 1800s, farmed lands by Hannaford and Barn, until, in partnership with Benjamin Hayman in 1806 (other records suggest 1809), he bought a tannery at Buckfastleigh and started woolcombing on a small scale. In 1818 Benjamin Hayman went out of business and Joseph continued alone.

Joseph Hamlyn had four children: Joseph, born 1807, John, born 1816, William, born 1822 and Susan. The three sons joined Joseph at an early age and it was through their combined efforts that the modern woollen industry came into being.

In 1842 the family rented the West Mill factory and, a few years later, bought the Town Mill (formerly called Sages). Here they installed the first combing machine which was to alter life considerably in Buckfastleigh. For, with the advent of machinery other master combers in Buckfastleigh were forced out of business. However, without machinery the woollen industry would not have survived. Certainly, it was thanks to the enterprise of the Hamlyns and the Berry's, who bought Buckfast Mill, that Buckfastleigh became the flourishing centre for the woollen industry.

Altogether, there were three mills in the town at this time: the Town Mill, West Mill and Churchward's Mill soon, unhappily, to be destroyed by fire. There were also two in Buckfast, of course, and the tannery.

Each of the sons of Joseph Hamlyn and, in turn, the grandsons, contributed in many ways to the growth and development of Buckfastleigh, industrially, socially and spiritually, being not only keen and enterprising business men but active in church and public life.

Of Joseph Hamlyn senior's four children, Joseph, his namesake, was the eldest. He was born in 1807 and died, unmarried, at the age of 81 years in 1888. Apparently he was a tall, good looking man, who managed the Hamlyn Bros. woollen mills at Horrrabridge until it was destroyed by fire in 1868 after which he retired.

John, the second son, born in 1816, was a man also considerably well thought of and probably most remembered because of his contribution both financially and personally to the building of the Totnes, Buckfastleigh and Ashburton Railway. He was its first chairman and continued so until his death in 1878. John was the son who built Fullaford House in 1876 but lived only two years to enjoy it.

William, the youngest son, who was born in 1882, had six sons and three daughters from his marriage to Mary, daughter of James Hamlyn of Holne in 1847. Four of those sons, James, John, William and Joseph played a continuing and important part in the life and development of Buckfastleigh; all of them achieving important positions in industry, local government and social organisations. It is these four sons whom older residents of Buckfastleigh may still remember:

JAMES (1847–1929) built Bossell Park. He was married to Sarah Petrie. He was a J.P., was active in business, politics and in church life and will probably be remembered most as the first member representing Buckfastleigh on the Devon County Council.

Mr. and Mrs. James Hamlyn (James, 1847–1929, son of William Hamlyn).

JOHN (1849–1898) inherited Fullaford from his uncle John (1816–1878) where he lived until he died. He, too, was a keen business man and an enthusiastic horse racer and hunter. He married twice, first, Mary Stranger Furneaux, in 1874 and then Jane Hoare and had children by both wives.

JOSEPH (1851–1932) he, too, had a love for Fullaford, which he bought on John's death. Like his brother he was a keen business man and a keen horse racer. He married Elizabeth Green, daughter of Henry Hamling (a distant connection) in 1874 and they had two daughters.

WILLIAM (1852). His home was Hapstead House. He married Ethel Shorrock Ashton by whom three of his children were Douglas, Joan and Ashton. He was extremely involved in public affairs and his duties included being a J.P. and chairman of the School Board. It was William who successfully negotiated the sale of the woollen mills to the Cooperative Wholesale Society in 1922. Other children included Thomas (1855) who lived in New Zealand for many years until he retired to Park View in Buckfastleigh; Hugh who emigrated to the U.S.A. and raised a family there; and three daughters Ann Maria, Emma Maude and Amy Beatrice. Amy married an F. Maddox and was responsible for the building of Cleavehurst. She died in 1931.

Joan Hamlyn (daughter of William and Ethel) I mention because she died only recently. She was the great granddaughter of the Joseph Hamlyn who farmed by Barn and Hannaford. Miss Hamlyn lived for many years at Ottery St. Mary and it was she who lent me the records from which I have been able to piece together the family history. Unfortunately, I never met her but it is with some notes that she made in 1961 at Ottery St. Mary that I want to conclude this chapter on the Hamlyn family.

"Father (William) often mentioned that Dawnton, often spoken of as Hamlyn property, was in the old days a large estate in Buckfastleigh, a parish which is now the separate, small estate of Brook Manor, Button Hapstead (our home) and possibly Bowerdon. The only proof of this is old maps, and, as I remember as a child, easy to follow paths which led from Bowerdon through Hapstead on to Button and into the woods at Brook. The old farm at Hapstead, where our tenants lived, was obviously the remains of an old manor house (examined and discussed by the Devon Association which traced the walls of a much bigger house) . . .

"Hapstead was said at one time to have been the rest house for the monks of Buckfast Abbey on their trips across the moors to Buckland and Tavistock . . . .

"Father owned a good deal of land around Buckfast and had given to my brother, Douglas, the old farm at Grange with its tithe barn. Bit by bit for financial reasons the lands were sold for building the many houses that there are now at Buckfast; and, I regret to say, that after my father's death, my brother Ashton was obliged to sell Hapstead . . . and Douglas sold Grange . . . so, as landowners we no longer exist, but I still feel that I belong to Devon and to the good earth of it."

There are now no Hamlyns living in Buckfastleigh.

Chapter Five

THE WARRENS AND THE HUNTS

IT IS not only the big landowners and gentry who contribute to the life and development of a town but the families with smaller businesses who, perhaps, come into contact with other local people regularly. It is these families who are remembered with affection—even many years later such as the Warrens and the Hunts.

The Warren family were well known woolcombers in the eighteenth century and their life and history could have been lost to us except that there are Warrens still living in Buckfastleigh today who are as well known as their ancestors were before them. Not only well known but well loved, too, for Marjorie Warren was a schoolteacher for a good number of years at Buckfastleigh Primary School; and her sister, Edith Walters, active in both social and church life. I have talked with both Miss Warren and Mrs. Walters, now retired, and, together with information received from Helen Harris, writer and niece of the Warrens, I can introduce you to the life and history of the Warren family.

Mrs. Harris says that the name Warren is believed to be derived from a De Warrenne who came to England with William the Conqueror in 1066, but this source may not be the sole origin of the name which occurs fairly widely throughout the country and in Devon, particularly around the Plymouth and elsewhere in the south.

Buckfastleigh parish register shows the name *Warren* or *Warrin* occurring at least from the seventeenth century with John a favoured christian name. The first lead we have is of John and Mary Warren one of whose younger children was William born in 1783. He became a tailor and married a woman also named Mary. One or two of his brothers were also woolcombers so it is possible that it was a family business. William and Mary appear to have had six children: Mary, 1810; Agnes, 1812; Frances, 1814; John, 1819; William, 1821 and Elizabeth Ellen, 1829. Of these, John, who was Helen Harris' great grandfather, was a woolcomber and stapler which suggests that he may have followed his uncles in the family firm.

Warren's Court, in Buckfastleigh, originally belonged to the Warrens and much of their work was carried on there. However, with the introduction of machinery the Warrens were put out of business like many other smaller concerns and, instead, Helen Harris' great grandfather, John, became a sadler and harness maker and is described in White's Directory as such.

In this latter business John was followed by his son, John William Warren, 1859–1940, who was one of eight children. Of these eight children the four eldest died in the diptheria epidemic of 1856 at the respective ages of six, four, two and one, a few days before the fifth child was born. Helen's grandfather, John William Warren, mentioned above, was, of course, the father of Marjorie Warren and Edith Walters.

Marjorie and Edith both remember their childhood and school days very clearly. They attended Buckfastleigh Primary School in the days when Mr. Abbot was head teacher before gaining scholarships to a school in Newton Abbot. In 1912 Marjorie went to a college in Bristol to train as a teacher and has been a teacher ever since. Her first two posts were in Sussex where she stayed until 1932 before returning to Buckfastleigh to teach in the Primary School where she taught for twenty-five years until her retirement in 1957. "I finished where I started," said Miss Warren. She added that ex-pupils still came up to her in the street; even people who were evacuees in the town during the war and had returned to Buckfastleigh for a holiday.

Edith Walters said she had spent most of her life with her parents at home; but, besides caring for them, has been actively involved with the parish church where she played the organ and taught in the Sunday School for over seventy years. Edith was responsible for starting the Women's section of the St. John's Ambulance Brigade; and was leader of the Buckfastleigh Amateur Dramatic Society's orchestra from its commencement. Edith is married to Mr. Frederick Walters.

Mr. Eddy Hunt's family came to Buckfastleigh from Chumleigh about 1795 and, like the Warrens and other families, were involved in the woollen industry.

After the Crimean War in 1855 the Hunt family who, at that time, lived at the lower end of Market Street near the River Mardle, suffered considerable losses and were forced to take up another kind of trade. The property was then used as a small holding, dairy and coal merchants. The family consisted of Susannah, Thomas, John, Lewis (who was Eddy's father) and William who later emigrated to New Zealand and was responsible for building most of the old part of Timaru in the South Island.

John Hunt married a Miss Shute and it was as a result of this marriage that the Hunts went into the bakery business at 71, Fore Street and John Hunt became a baker.

Before the Co-operative Wholesale Society opened in 1869 in the early parts of the nineteenth century there were several bakers shops in Buckfastleigh. Times were hard and there was competition to survive among the traders but the Hunts survived by extending their service to include the delivery of bread to country districts.

When John retired he went to live at Wood View in Plymouth Road with his wife. Thomas, who was living away from Buckfastleigh at the time, took over the bakery from John and eventually Lewis came down from Market Street in 1905 and took it over. The business, in the Hunts name, lasted from the early 1800s to 1969 and the family business is well remembered by Buckfastleigh folk, as are the family themselves who had a close and continuing association with the Congregational Church.

Lewis and his wife, Margaret (nee Saunders), had two sons, John and Eddy and three daughters, Mabel (married to Albert James Stone, manager of the C.W.S.); Emmeline (married to Frederick Walters R.N.) and Edith. When Lewis took over the business many of the bakeries in the town had closed down. Eventually, the Hunts took over the Shutes business when the elder son, John, married and went to live there.

Lewis died in 1939 and the business was taken over by John, Eddy and Edith. Eddy, his wife, Minnie, and Edith running the lower shop doing catering as well; and Jack and his wife, Winifred, running the top shop.

Eddy Hunt remembers with relish the bread in the early days. "We heated the oven with wood faggots," he said. "Wood was brought in from Hembury Wood and each year there were sales of wood which were held at the *Sun Inn*. The wood was brought in acres and then bundled into faggots which, when used, were put right into the oven. This gives the bread a lovely taste", said Eddy. Now, of course, Henbury Woods is in the hands of the National Trust. Lewis looked after Hembury Woods for a number of years and was offered the first chance of buying it which he reluctantly turned down.

Now in his eighties, Eddy Hunt, looking back on many memories, including two world wars, lives with his nephew and niece, Mr. Gordon and Miss Muriel Stone, in Fore Street. Eddy's sister, Mabel, was their mother.

Mr. and Miss Stone have many memories of their youth, too, partly spent living with their grandfather, Lewis Hunt, at the lower Fore Street bakery. Both Mr. and Miss Stone were teachers and Gordon is now a town councillor. John's two sons, John and Martin, followed other professions. John is on the staff of Leylands and Martin is a quantity surveyor.

John Russell Hunt still lives and plays an active part in Buckfastleigh life. He is Thomas Hunt's grandson and the son of John (painter and decorator).

Mr. Eddy Hunt in military uniform of the First World War. *Courtesy of Mr. E. Hunt.*

Messrs. John and Eddy Hunt outside their bakers' shop, Fore Street, in the 1950s. *Courtesy of Mr. E. Hunt.*

Chapter Six
DEVELOPMENT IN BUCKFASTLEIGH
THE METHODIST CHURCH

ALTHOUGH Buckfast was essentially a Roman Catholic stronghold (in spite of the fact that in the middle of the nineteenth century Buckfast Abbey still lay in ruins) and Buckfastleigh people very attached to Holy Trinity Parish Church, restored in 1844, non-conformism thrived!

Two Wesleyan chapels were in use before the present Methodist church was built in 1834. The earlier one, now demolished, was in Chapel Street, on a site opposite the C.W.S. store; and, the other one also recently demolished, was made into the Mill office (a little further up the street). However, it appears that the very first meeting place of the Wesleyans was where Wakeham's Dairy used to be, practically opposite the Y.M.C.A.

Joseph Hamlyn, the elder, Christoper Furneaux of Hapstead, John Butchers the tanner, William Tucker, the schoolmaster, Walter Soper, of Buckfast, and later, Thomas Winsor of High Beara farm and John Barnes of Kilbury all contributed to the rise of Methodism in Buckfastleigh.

Although it does not appear that John Wesley, the evangelist, ever visited Buckfastleigh, he certainly visited Ashburton on 31st August in 1776. Apparently, he was accosted by a mob which did not give him a good impression of local people. However, it did not stop Ashburton and Buckfastleigh becoming a stronghold for Methodism.

Before the turn of the eighteenth century Ashburton and Buckfastleigh were in the South Devon circuit. In 1803, through the work of one of John Wesley's preachers, William Thoresby, the Ashburton circuit was formed which included Ashburton, Buckfastleigh, Bovey Tracey, Wolston Green and other places.

THE CONGREGATIONAL CHURCH

It was nearly seventy years later that the foundation stone of the Congregational Church was laid on the site of the old "chapple" house which had been bought for £90 in 1798. However, the Congregational Church ministry had begun almost two hundred years previously in 1672 when King Charles II had issued a licence allowing the market house in the town to be used for non-conformist worship. A former Puritan minister in Denbury, who had been deprived of his living at the Restoration, was taken out of retirement and installed as the first minister of Buckfastleigh.

BUCKFASTLEIGH PRIMARY SCHOOL

The (old) schoolroom was the scene of great industriousness each weekday as schoolmasters and mistresses attempted to instil some knowledge into the often unwilling heads of the boys and girls from Buckfastleigh and the surrounding area.

It is interesting to look back on the records of Buckfastleigh school to see how humbly it began and how the master and children had to put up with inadequate premises, inadequate materials and inadequate help.

In the middle of the nineteenth century it was not every child's privilege to attend school. Many were forced to work, most probably in the Mill, to bring in some money to help feed the family. Some children worked part-time and attended school the rest of the week.

The first qualified or certificated teacher appears to have been William Parker. By law he was required to keep a log book and make daily entries of anything which "might deserve to be recorded". I have printed a few entries from these records which are enlightening and interesting. Both girls and boys studied together at this time and were not separated until much later in the development of the school's history (before finally becoming mixed again).

12th March, 1868. The following report received this morning: The First Standard passed badly, the Third Standard exceedingly well. In the 2nd Standard Arithmetic is weak and in the 4th Standard there were some failures in spelling. The 5th Standard passed very well, taken as a whole and, considering this is my first inspection of the school under a certified teacher, the results are most encouraging. Order is good but the tendency to copying should be stringently repressed. The reading book should be better graduated and a paid monitor should be engaged.

It was signed by John Furneaux.

26th May, 1870. Parents seem to expect us to let their children do just as they like, as they do at home, and get offended if we attempt a proper system of discipline and withdraw them in a passion. Find it very difficult to deal with such people.

February, 1871. A meeting of ratepayers is called for next Tuesday to decide about having School Board for the town.

8th February, 1871. We were abused by one of the girl's mother's today for not giving the child a prize.

14th February, 1871. It was unanimously resolved today at the ratepayers meeting to have a School Board. The next inspection by John Furneaux leads him to write in his report:

> My Lords have paid the full grant this year but they will be unable to continue the grant any longer unless an improvement is made in the lighting of the room, to the darkness of which the H.M. Inspector called attention in his last report. The drainage must at once be improved. . . .

18th January, 1873. The Girls' School has opened this week and thirty-four of our girls are transferred to it leaving our school thinly occupied at present.

In 1875 the new school was erected at a cost of £2,959. Other schools built at this time were Coombe in 1886, Buckfast R.C. school in 1893 and Buckfast in 1894.

From a report written in 1885 it was clear that a new master had taken over, Alfred G. Abbot, a certificated master (2nd class).

The present master has been charge for two months and seems likely to improve the condition of the school. . . .

Alfred George Abbot was a man much respected in the town and a schoolmaster still remembered by some of Buckfastleigh's "Old Boys". He lived in the school house, married twice and was not only a schoolmaster but a deputy registrar of marriage too. He was a religious man and a staunch Methodist and is as much remembered for his church activities as his school work.

Mr. Alfred G. Abbott.

Mr. Eddy Hunt of Fore Street, now in his eighties, remembers him well. He also remembers his old school mates, Aubrey Bennett, Bert Abbot, Bill Roberts, Alfred Callard and Edgar Reed (who was a bit younger).

Mr. Stanley Harris, now retired, remembers Mr. Abbot with affection. "Although Mr. Abbot stammered he made life interesting to boys," said Stanley, "but none of us really appreciated him until later," he added.

"It's funny," continued Stanley, "the little things you remember. In those days the school was mixed up to a certain age before boys and girls separated (this would be in the early years before the First World War). When I first went to school we sat in a gallery, we didn't have desks and chairs. We wrote on slates with slate pencils. When we were called from the infants to the seniors, there were six of us, we had to walk from one end of the school to the other. One boy decided to be the spokesman and when he knocked on the door of the senior school Mr. Abbot answered. 'Please Sir,' the boy began, 'Us be come.' Now why does that stick in my memory?" laughed Stanley Harris.

As far as Buckfastleigh School is concerned it was set on its course with a high standard of work and discipline and caring. Hundreds of Buckfastleigh people have passed through the caring hands of the staff of this school. Not many people living today would have known Alfred Abbot, but there are many who would remember Marjorie Warren mentioned earlier in the book (including myself for she was my teacher, too), and latterly Mr. A. W. Thompson, headmaster, who now lives in Buckfast.

Today, in the 1980s, Buckfastleigh Primary School, headed by Mr. J. W. Shinner, has ten teaching staff caring for 300 children. It caters for children between the ages of 5 and 11 and, in the words of the school, its aim "is to provide an educational environment which is happy, interesting and suited to the individual needs of each child. As a priority we are concerned about *basic* language (speech, reading and writing) and mathematics . . ." and, "other areas of educational activity are not neglected; religious instruction, social studies, art, music, drama, physical education and games are all an important part of the broad curriculum we try to provide."

A physical training display in Victoria Park during the 1930s. *Courtesy of Mrs. E. Walters.*

A production of The Lacemakers. Who among this group of 1920 schoolchildren do you recognise besides Mrs. Mabel Pearden, Susie Petherbridge and Gwen O'Brien? *Courtesy of Mrs. O'Brien and Mr. E. Beer.*

Buckfastleigh pupils in 1939. If you do not recognise the children you may recognise the teachers — Miss Marjorie Warren, Mrs. Jackson, Mrs. Midgley and Mrs. Scoble. *Courtesy of Miss M. Warren.*

THE BUCKFASTLEIGH CO-OPERATIVE SOCIETY

A little book called, *The Buckfastleigh Cooperative Society Ltd. Jubilee History (1869–1919)*, by Mr. J. Dyer, tells the story of the commencement of the C.W.S. in Buckfastleigh in 1869 and its growth over the next 50 years.

". . . the credit of starting a co-operative store was principally due to Messrs. Thos. Easterbrook and Geoffrey Prowse with its first member being Mr. John Furneaux of Higher Town." The same John Furneaux, no doubt, who was so active in the affairs of Buckfastleigh School. The C.W.S. has played a significant part in the life of Buckfastleigh due to a number of local people who believed in the co-operative system and worked hard to make it a success.

It started in a shop in Fore Street, right opposite the Post Office and its first night's takings were 2/6½d. (It was only open four nights a week then). Nine years later in 1878 the Grocery store was built on the site where the C.W.S. shops still stand with the Bakery opening in 1884, and the Butchery Dept. in 1887. With a few set backs the C.W.S. continued to expand until in 1970 the Society acquired the Hamlyn Mills.

One person who made a significant contribution to the C.W.S. was Mr. James Dyer of Plymouth Road, Buckfastleigh, who was born in Forder Green, Broadhempston. His daughter, Mrs. Gwen O'Brien, who still lives in Plymouth Road, told me that James was one of nine children whose father died after he was kicked by a cow. Harriet, James' mother, used to go to work on a nearby farm to do a day's washing for 6d and a jug of milk to help support her large family. Finally, young James' sisters went into an orphanage and James and his brother, Bill, went to live on their grandparents' farm, Red Post, between Totnes and Newton Abbot. But life was strict with the grandparents, said Gwen O'Brien, and it was, "Dogs to doors and boys to bed," at eight every evening! This was too much for these adolescent boys used to more freedom; but the final crunch came when Bill was asked to skin a dead sheep! He ran away leaving James with the grandparents.

Eventually, James Dyer went to work for a man called Coffee Smith, at the Livery Stables in Buckfastleigh; and, by fifteen years of age was driving the mail cart.

Gwen's mother, who lived in Higher Town, got to know young James Dyer (who then lived in Newton Abbot) when he was marooned in Buckfastleigh during the great blizzard of 1891. They courted for nine years and after they married lived in Higher Town and it was during this period that James became a postman doing the Rattery round.

On August 7th 1907, James Dyer was elected to the committee of the C.W.S. and, after long service, during which he contracted and recovered from tuberculosis, he was elected President and remained so for fourteen years.

Mr. J. Dyer with colleagues in postman's uniforms during the early part of this century. *Courtesy of Mr. F. Paddon and Mr. E. Beer.*

Mrs. Gwen O'Brien, daughter of John Dyer, as a young woman in 1933. *Courtesy of Mrs. O'Brien and Mr. E. Beer.*

Chapter Seven

THE REED FAMILY AND BUCKFASTLEIGH

ANOTHER grocery and provision store, still in existence today, belongs to the Reed family of Buckfastleigh. It is a much smaller concern than the C.W.S. stores, of course, but equally successful and was a going concern long before the Co-operative stores were started.

In 1854 John Reed (1829-1915) married Elizabeth Parson Rice (1834-1896). They had twelve children, six girls and six boys of whom John Leonard Reed was the sixth child. In 1872 when John Leonard was eight years old the family came to live in Market Street, Buckfastleigh, from Petherton, in Devon, and their descendants have lived in the house and have run a grocery and provision store since that time — 109 years.

The business which John and Elizabeth Reed took over in 1872 had originally belonged to Julia Shapter. Julia's husband, Edward Shapter, a tailor, had bought three dwelling houses belonging to John Tinckham, Richard Eales, Peter Corkney, James Easterbrook, John Worth and John Tonkin for £150 in 1788. When Edward died, the property was left in trust for Julia who set up the business. On her death, John Shapter, her son, took it over but eventually moved to Plymouth and John Furneaux rented the business until 1872 when John Reed came to Buckfastleigh.

As a young man young John Leonard Reed worked in the shop with his family for a while. By then the shop sold tobacco and snuff and had also acquired a licence for the sale of wines and spirits. Eventually he grew restless and went to work as a traveller in Kingsbridge, returning to live in Buckfastleigh at a later date.

John Leonard married Annie Foot, born 1868 in Ashburton, and they had three children, the oldest being Edgar Reed, born Kingsbridge 1898, to whom the family business eventually came. He and his wife Sybil had four children, Bobby, born 1932, Janet, born 1935, Timothy, born 1937 and Jimmy, born 1946. On retiring Edgar passed the business on to his son, Timothy, who runs it as a flourishing concern. Although Edgar is retired from business he is still active socially and has an impressive record behind him. He is particularly well known for his caving exploits.

A family group showing Mr. E. Reed, as a small boy, with his father, John L. Reed (centre) in 1900.

BUCKFASTLEIGH CAVES

Buckfastleigh possesses magnificent limestone caves which are the home of bats and invaluable prehistoric finds of bones belonging to giant deer, rhinoceros, elephants, cave lions, wild cats, hyenas, bears, wolves, foxes and badgers and the tooth of a sabre-tooth tiger dating back 100,000 years.

In 1937 Edgar Reed and "Squeak" Joint, another well known local man discovered three caves not previously known. One of them was subsequently named Reed's cave, is complete with beautiful formations. In the second cave the men discovered bones which they sent to a natural history museum for identification. The museum wrote back saying they were of no value but, fortunately, friends of Edgar's were not satisfied and the bones were sent to the British Museum.

The bones had been found under six inches of stalagmite indicating that they were at least 10,000 years old. The British Museum wrote back immediately to say that the finds were important and that the caves should be closed immediately. Although the discovery of Reed's cave was publicised the discovery of the cave where the bones were found was kept secret until further excavations had been completed.

Edgar remembers being trapped in one of the caves when, in 1939 in company with Squeak Joint and others, they squeezed through the narrow entrance into the cave.

"When you go into a cave," said Edgar, "Your clothes become wet, rucked up and stretched. When I came to get out of the cave I couldn't manage it. It worried me because it was the only exit from the cave. In the end I had to take all my clothes off and slide out!"

At the entrance to the cave there used to be two cow sheds, complete with a foot of cow dung, today there is an excellent museum. The sheds were ripped out and concreted by volunteers who came to Buckfastleigh during their holidays over a period of four years. Through various generous donations in time, money and material, the museum was completed and during the summer period it has been known for over 2,000 visitors to visit the cave in a fortnight. "There is still quite a bit of work to be done," Edgar told me, "and, at present, two rooms are being made into laboratories for students who want to do research."

The land originally belonged to the Coulton family. When the Coultons decided to sell the land in 1961, including the quarry area in which the caves are situated, it was felt that the area was so important and unique that the British Museum wrote to the Society for the Preservation of Nature Reserves which bought the top field over the quarries, the quarry where the caves are and the surrounding fields. Then the S.P.N.R. handed the caves over to the Devon Trust for the Preservation of Nature Reserves which, in turn, passed the responsibility to Buckfastleigh which manages the caves on behalf of the preservation society. The Devon Speliogical Society was formed in 1947. Edgar Reed was elected president and has remained so ever since.

Edgar Reed in Easter chamber, Reed's cave, 1939.

Easter chamber, Reed's cave, Buckfastleigh.

Chapter Eight
THE COULTON FAMILY AND THE BUCKFASTLEIGH RACES

THE COULTON family who, prior to 1962, owned the land on which the Buckfastleigh caves are situated also have a long connection with Dean and Buckfastleigh. For many generations they were tenants of Dean Court Farm, part of Lord Churston's estate, mentioned earlier in the book, arriving first in 1836 to farm neighbouring lands. Mr. Edward Coulton, who lives with his wife, Eileen, in Plymouth Road, told me that his grandfather, William Richard Coulton, who owned considerable property around Buckfastleigh was one of the main initiators of the Buckfastleigh Races in 1884 together with a group of local sportsmen.

"The first race," said Mr. Coulton, "was held on Wallaford Down in 1883." The following year saw the racecourse set up properly on Dean Marshes, the Coulton's farm and Lord Churston's land. Joseph Hamlyn was the first president of the Buckfastleigh Race Committee and his two horses, *All Fours* and *Caprice*, won about fifty races. Before the turn of the century the Races became recognised under National Hunt Rules and the town continued to enjoy its races until 1960 when the National Hunt meetings finished when Lord Churston sold his lands. However, racing in Buckfastleigh was far from finished and a site beside the busy A38 road was rented for "point to point" racing for many years afterwards.

Mr. Edward Coulton remembers well his childhood days in Buckfastleigh especially his school days. One of seven surviving children, of whom he is the eldest, he attended first a private school run by Miss Tucker, daughter of the then Vicar of Buckfastleigh and held at the Vicarage in the early days of the twentieth century. Then he attended the Buckfastleigh Council School for a short time before going to Totnes Grammar School. He left school at the age of thirteen years in 1916 and started working on the farm with his father, Edward James Coulton, who also, in his time, had been secretary of the Buckfastleigh Race Course Committee.

In 1916 labour was in short supply as local men had gone to fight in the Great War. Edward stayed with his father, until four years after his marriage in 1927 when he moved to Staverton to farm. He remained in Staverton for most of his working life returning to Buckfastleigh to retire after he had handed over the Staverton farm to his son. His brother, John (Jack) Coulton had stayed on at Dean Farm until the day came when Lord Churston decided to sell the land. This meant the end of the races, of course. Some land was sold to tenants and some by public auction. Jack Coulton decided that this was the time to make a move and the farm was sold.

Chapter Nine
THE REBUILDING OF BUCKFAST ABBEY

IN 1884 the rebuilding of Buckfast Abbey began and the foundations laid on the site of the twelfth century building. Two years earlier in 1882 a group of French Benedictine monks who had belonged to a community founded by a pious French priest, Pere Muard, at Pierre-qui-Vire, near Dijon, came to England and made their foundation at Buckfast.

The monks had lived an enclosed life of a most austere and rigid kind. The monks who had taken Holy Orders spent their lives preaching the gospel; and the laybrothers spent their days on work of different kinds.

I spoke to our present day Abbot, Father Leo Smith, who said that it is against the background of their concept of monastic life that the rebuilding of the Abbey on its mediaeval foundations was begun. The life at Buckfast was strict and the emphasis was on manual work. He said that it was this that enabled them to undertake the gigantic task.

When the French monks returned to their mother house in France at the repeal of the penal laws, recruitment for Buckfast Abbey was from South Germany. It was the German monks who did the main rebuilding especially since the link with La Pierre-qui-Vire was broken when the Abbey became independent in 1902.

In 1902 Dom Boniface Natter became the first Abbot of Buckfast since the Reformation, but his unfortunate death in the shipwreck of the *Sirio*, off Cartagena in August, 1906, ended his rule of Buckfast. He was succeeded by Dom Anscar Vonier and it was the new Abbot who proclaimed his intention to rebuild the ancient Abbey Church which began in 1907.

Part Three
IN LIVING MEMORY

Chapter Ten

A PICTURE OF BUCKFASTLEIGH

AT THE turn of the century and during the years leading up to the First World War times were hard for local people and poverty was common among many of the hard working families in Buckfastleigh. Miss Stone, of Fore Street, told me that her aunt, Edith Hunt, remembered people sneaking across to the tannery to scrape meat off the sheep-skins in order to keep themselves alive; and Edgar Reed remembers a man who pinched an ox-hide from the Mill. He had hidden it in the gap between the walls of his home. He was the last man to be sent to Australia from Buckfastleigh as a convict.

The coming of machinery had already altered the social and economic situation in Britain generally and the effects were felt no less keenly in places like Buckfastleigh; for with poor living conditions, hard and difficult winters and poor wages, fewer spinning and weaving jobs traditionally done in people's homes must have added to the misery of many of the inhabitants of Buckfastleigh.

In the winter of 1891 fierce snow storms swept the South-West and most of the towns and villages in South Devon were completely cut off. Elderly local inhabitants I have spoken to still talk of the *Year of the Blizzard*, and Moore, the photographer, took a photograph of Fore Street several inches deep in snow which, in many cases, came up to the bedroom windows of some of the smaller cottages.

The great blizzard of 1891 showing part of Fore Street under several feet of snow. *Courtesy of Mrs. E. Walters and Miss M. Warren.*

However, although times were hard people still managed to enjoy themselves. In those days fairs still came to the town and Glovers Park, now all housing, was once a field where cattle markets were held until they closed just before the First World War.

Miss Connie James remembers other social occasions such as the Wednesday night socials held in the Methodist Church hall, run by Miss Joan Hamlyn and dancing classes where they used to plait the maypole.

On 5th November bonfires were lit on Barter's Bridge at the bottom of Fore Street and local children used to steal wood to put on the bonfire. When they were chastised by the local policeman, one year, said Connie James, they threatened to put him on the bonfire, too!

Netta Tonkin, who lives in Fore Street, was born Annetta Carolyne Rice in 1894 and grew up in a family who owned a bakery. When I talked with her she told me about the living conditions of the day when many families had no oven and local bakers used to bake their Sunday dinners for them, "Not only their joints, but their potatoes, onions and carrots, too," she said.

People who worked out at Buckfast and had to leave home at 5.30 in the morning often came into the bakers for some dough which they could make up into flat buns called "hobbins" and which they could take with them to eat for their breakfasts.

Most mill workers had to start early in those days. Mrs. Edith Walters told me that the Hamlyns employed a man who would go round to the homes of employees very early in the morning and wake them up by banging a long stick on their bedroom windows!

Cottages were small and it was common for five or six in a family to live in one tiny cottage. Connie James, who lives in a cottage over 300 years old, told me that her grandmother, "Granny Roberts", brought up a family of eight in it. She also told me that her family have lived in the cottage, in Elliots Cross, for ninety-seven years.

Of the town itself Mr. Edward Coulton remembers when parts of Chapel Street were only wide enough for a horse and cart. "There were three cottages opposite the C.W.S. building in Chapel Street then," he said. "And when cars were first seen on the road people used to run to the hedge to stare at them as they passed by".

Shops and their owners have come and gone and Mr. Coulton remembers only Edgar Reed's shop still belonging to the same family as it did when he was a boy.

Connie James surprised me with her memory for she could name most of the shops in Fore Street and their owners as far back as 1914 at least. Other older inhabitants may still remember them, too. Starting from Weech Corner and going down to Barter's Bridge there were on the left and right hand side of the road:

Hoskins *Furniture and undertakers*	Fosters
Mr. Butchers, China	Gillard's Woolshop
Wattons, Milk and Papers	Chaffes, *tobacconist*
Shaw's, Fruit	Bradfords, Groceries
Searles, Newsagents	Cousins, Chemist
Georges' Jewellery	Shutes, Bakery
Petherbridges	Barretts, Butchers
Post Office	Coods, Bakery
Hunts	Rices, Bakery
Sweet shop	Penny, Jewellery
Warrens, Saddlery	Hunts, Bakery
Luckrafts, Ironmongery	Hoares, Butchers
	Maria Lane, Groceries
	Gillards, Boots shop
	Moores, Photographers

The station tree in 1935 which unfortunately has long gone.

The only Victorian postbox left in Buckfastleigh outside Reed's grocer shop in Market Street. *Courtesy of Mr. J. Allen.*

View of Fore Street during the early part of this century. *Courtesy of Mrs. E. Walters and Miss M. Warren.*

Dean Prior showing the old road (no traffic!) with one man ready for work and two children dressed in their best Sunday clothes. *Courtesy of Mrs. E. Walters.*

The local hunt starting off from Dean Prior will certainly bring back memories of this and similar meets. Taken between the wars the hounds are off to a good start. *Courtesy of Mrs. E. Walters.*

One shop owner well remembered by older inhabitants was Tom Luckraft who was born in 1845 and who died in 1921. During his lifetime he was known as a plumber, ironmonger and blacksmith in Fore Street; but he was also one of the pioneers of electricity in the town, experimenting on his own initiative with some success.

Many people who remember Buckfastleigh railway station before it was closed down and bought privately will remember Station Tree (a beautiful horse chestnut) and the seat around it. The seat was donated by Tom Luckraft in commemoration of Queen Victoria's Jubilee. Now, neither the tree nor the seat remain.

Stanley Harris of Bossell Road remembers Tom Luckraft well: "He was a plumber" said Stanley, also a plumber for most of his life, "With his workshop right over the brook, by the corner of Fore Street and Elliot's Plain, he used to mend tin kettles, for he was a tinsmith too as plumbers often were in those days. He hammered away from Monday to Saturday." "Not many houses had plumbing then," remembered Stanley, "and few houses had toilets or baths."

Because of the woollen industry water has been an important factor in the development of Buckfastleigh. But water which is fit for washing wool is not necessarily fit for human consumption.

In about 1890 the locality suffered from typhoid epidemics which medical opinion attributed to the fact that certain families kept pigs within a few feet of their houses and wells, which were then a sole source of drinking water. It was again the Hamlyn family, James and William, who approached the Totnes Local Authority which resulted in a small water supply being brought in and swine forbidden to be allowed near.

Under provision of the Local Government Act in 1884 the original parish was divided into East and West, the former governed by an Urban District Council of nine members, established in 1894 with William Hamlyn as its first chairman. He lost no time in pressing for an extensive sewerage system which was completed as quickly as possible with the water scheme following. Apparently, the Buckfastleigh death rate, formerly 22 per 1000, was reduced to 10.

Leslie Lane of Harewood, who for many years worked at the Buckfastleigh reservoir, told me that there were many water leats in the town, one being found at the top of Silver Street where people obtained water for washing. There was also a tap in Jordan Street and by the *Sun Inn*, and, on Sundays, in the old days, he told me, men used to collect water for their wives to do the washing on Mondays. The water came from the old tin mines and the men carried home the buckets of water on their shoulders. Eventually, of course, the reservoir was built and Joseph Hamlyn, who had acquired the site of the reservoir, handed over his rights as a gift to the town on condition he had a supply to his house (Fullaford) for domestic use. A brass plate was affixed to a brick pillar at the reservoir stating this condition, but eventually this was stolen. The land on which the reservoir was built previously belonged to Mr. E. Churchward of Hillside, Buckfastleigh.

Having mentioned the *Sun Inn* I can go no further without mentioning the other inns and taverns in the town many of which have now closed down. They were: *The Town Arms, The Tradesman Arms, The Royal Oak, The Golden Lion, The Bridge Inn, The Commercial, The Valiant Soldier, The Prince of Wales, The Half Moon* (now *The Stable Door*), *The Globe, The Kings Arms, The Sun Inn, The White Hart, The Waterman's Arms*. Only the last six in this list still remain.

Although by this time the weekly market had ended, two fairs for cattle and wool were held on the third Thursday in June and the second Thursday in September. (Observant folk who walk Market Street will notice at intervals along the pavement little places where the hurdles were fixed to keep the cattle in. Later, the hurdles were found in the cottages in Chapel Street owned by John Allen of Bossell.)

The Factory Cottages (known generally as Weavers' Cottages) are well over 140 years old and were once owned by the Earl of Macclesfield who lived at Brook Manor. However, in the latter half of the nineteenth century, the corner cottage was turned into a sweet shop called Smiths. The next cottage was also a sweet shop owned by a seafaring man and John Allen remembers being told that there was always a big jar in the window with jellied or conger eels in it to draw children's attention to the shop. Apparently there was great rivalry between the two shops!

View of the old factory cottages (known as Weavers' Cottages), in Chapel Street. *Courtesy of Mr. J. Allen.*

At this time Australia and America were becoming popular countries to which to emigrate and the following passages are taken from a letter written to Edgar Reed's father by Edgar's uncle when he emigrated to Australia at the end of the nineteenth century. It is a fascinating letter, all the more remarkable because of the courage it must have taken in those days to sail across to the other side of the world in conditions far more dangerous and uncomfortable than one has to face today when travelling.

Ship Harbinger,
13th July 18

My dear John,

I am endeavouring to write to each of you tho' I have little news when nearly all is written in notes, as there is little change on a sailing ship during voyage. It is a job to pass the time away pleasantly as it is too noisy to read or write. So, we pass the evening with games of whist, dominoes, chess, draughts, in fact, some are at it nearly all day; but I like, if possible, to get out during the day to get some fresh air. We cannot get much as there is little space to walk except on poop where only first class passengers are allowed, unless the decks are too wet and —————— dangerous when we second class are invited up, but generally, in that case, the quarter deck is covered with water so we can't get to poop unless we wade above deck. We have at times had the deck full of water, hundreds of tons of water, but fortunately she quickly emptied herself through scupper holes. We have had some near shaves of going down. The captain and seamen say they never experienced such rough weather but I hope it is all over now altho' it is freshening up again today and very cold wind. We have not sighted land since off Dungness and no ship near so we have had very little variety....

The best things to bring for second to third sailing and 3rd steamer is: deck chair, strip of carpet, some tins of sardines, extract of meat, lobster and salmon, bloater paste, tin of tongue, cake and biscuits, eggs, butter, sherbet, tins of rice, coeva, a small spirit lamp and kettle with spirit, bread, milk, pills, salts, (a course of medicine should be taken a few days before starting as it often prevents sickness). Brandy is good for staying stomachs when sick and essence of beef tea sustaining. A few nails, insect destroyer, camphor may be useful. Tea is alright if you bring a teapot. Dubbin is good for preserving boots from sea water.

I tell you this as it may be useful to you. I think I have put further information in my notes. It would be very pleasant on a sailing vessel if there was no drinking on it and provided one had average fair weather. We have had it exceptionally bad in the southern hemisphere and we are just told that they expect a "southern buster" tonight which is very comforting considering it is the worst quarter for a storm in these latitudes. I can tell you it is cold now blowing straight from the ice — and raining heavily. A chain just snapped which was holding down a jib sail and the sail flapped about making a noise like thunder and the chain flying about like paper was broken to pieces by knocking links against each other.

I suppose you are now enjoying summer weather and perhaps playing a cricket match. I hope you will have done well....

Women going third class should take thrashing board and brush. All take soap, towels, bedding, blacking, etc.

Anyone who cares for fishing might have an opportunity to catch a shark, dolphin or birds and should have a long line and large hooks. If you know anyone in Australia from Buckfastleigh you might send their addresses as I might call on them. I suppose there will be no letters awaiting me if we arrive in a fortnight as anticipated.

With love I remain,
Your affectionate brother,
(signed) Nathaniel.

A new life opened up for those fortunate in reaching their new destination. (Nathaniel was fortunate and succeeded in making a new life for himself in Australia.) However, most of Buckfastleigh's population had no desire to emigrate and stayed behind to live the life that they knew and understood.

Of course, there were not only those who left Buckfastleigh but those who came to live in the town. Such newcomers were called "sojourners". As part of the harsh Poor Law Act new inhabitants who became a liability, i.e. who could not find work and therefore had no money, were liable to be returned to the parish from which they had come. It is thought that a row of cottages in Market Street, next to the house used as the first (Congregational) Chapel for non-conformist worship, were kept as poor houses for those coming from the work house in Totnes.

In 1911 Buckfastleigh boasted three council schools in the parish and an Abbey school, a Town Hall, a well equipped Y.M.C.A. (with club rooms for girls, too), a public park with a band stand and a recreation ground for sporting activities. The town also boasted electricity. Of industry there were three woollen mills, a paper mill, iron foundry and tannery. Spiritually, the town was thriving, too, with the churches and Sunday Schools full.

The First World War, the Great War, must have inevitably changed the life and character of Buckfastleigh as it did in the rest of the country, with the bulk of the young men volunteering to fight the enemy leaving gaps in the industrial and social life of the town which many brave women attempted to fill.

The Buckfastleigh Co-operative Society by 1914, extending its services considerably, like other industries, lost a number of men to the armed forces. Not only men but a number of horses, too, were taken for war purposes. Suddenly, the new fangled machine, the motor car, came into its own and the C.W.S. purchased one, desperately needing some other form of transport for their goods. A garage was built on a piece of land adjoining the bakery and fitted out with an electric light, another recent innovation.

And what of the monks at Buckfast, engaged in the arduous rebuilding of the Abbey? There seems to have been a very good relationship with people in the early years, the Abbot told me. The monks ran the parishes and a number of families became Roman Catholic. But many of the monks were German and the outbreak of the war in 1914, with the bitterness and hatred of all that was German, seems to have broken the bond of friendship and it was not until the Second World War and its immediate aftermath that the barriers of suspicion began to come down.

As in other places, large houses were commandeered for various uses connected with service personnel. Bigadon House, owned by the Flemings and described as "the graceful old Adams House with ornate fireplaces" by the late journalist, Gertrude Weekes, was used as a convalescent home for officers.

A way of life had come to an end with the First World War. A loss of man power and an exodus of local men and women through migration to other countries but with a corresponding influx of people through marriage; the beginning of the liberation of women who had taken on many jobs and tasks hitherto primarily men's occupations meant a shift in the power and the balance of the population. Even the large family units, such as the Hamlyns had been affected and an era really came to an end when this family, so long the benefactors of Buckfastleigh who had played a major part in bringing most of the town's facilities into being, sold the Buckfastleigh Woollen Mills to the Co-operative Wholesale Society in 1920.

A gun used in the First World War on display in Fore Street during the same period. *Courtesy of Mr. F. Paddon and Mr. E. Beer.*

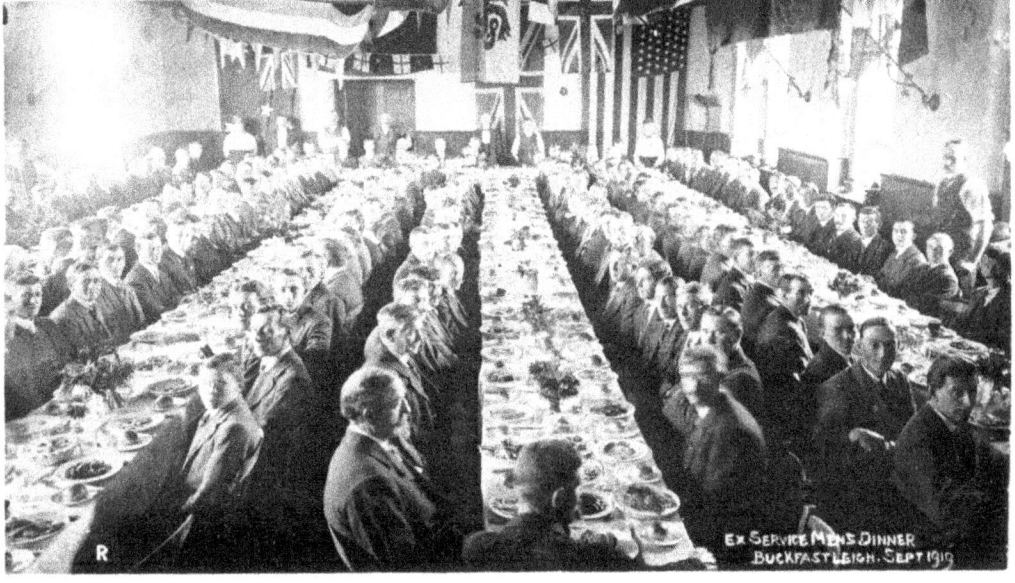

The First World War ex-servicemen's dinner held in the Town Hall in 1919. *Courtesy of Mrs. A. Callard and Mr. E. Beer.*

Chapter Eleven
BETWEEN THE TWO WARS

IN AN article on Buckfastleigh Gertrude Weekes wrote that after the First World War there was a flurry of building activity in Buckfastleigh with council housee being built at Buckfast, Glovers Park (1925) and West End (1928) and private builders building detached and semi-detached housing. In 1925–26 a wide arterial road was constructed between Exeter and Plymouth which meant that existing bridges had to be widened and strengthened and the bed of the river diverted. Tourist traffic started to flow and the first char-a-banc, owned by Messrs. Millman and Son, and the first buses, owned by Babingtons, which ran between Newton Abbot and Buckfastleigh, were seen on the road.

One very necessary service which has not yet been mentioned is the Buckfastleigh Fire Service started by Mr. Millman and Mr. Blackford in the early days of the twentieth century. Then, of course, horses (owned by the two men) were used to draw the fire fighting equipment. In 1912 a Merryweather engine, now a museum piece, was in use. Leslie Lane of Harewood, for many years a fireman, remembers his early days in the Fire Service when a steam engine was used and kept in Silver Street.

"After the horses," said Leslie, "Wakehams lorry and then the Co-op coal lorry was used to get to the fire. Only you had to get the lorry before you could get to the fire. The upright coal boiler had to be kept full of water and once the steam was up it would pump water," he said. "The boiler had to be lit whilst the lorry was racing to the fire. This meant that half of the coal was lost by the time the fire was reached by the *Iron Men* as the firemen were then called."

Leslie Lane, who still has in his possession part of a leather hose made in the time of the hand pumps and an old brass helmet worn before the modern ones came into use, was in the fire service for thirty years and received the Queen's Long Service medal.

A notable achievement came in 1922 when Buckfast Abbey was opened for worship by the devoted and hardworking monks who did not actually complete their task until 1938. Dom John Stephan says in his book on Buckfast Abbey that in 1922 the bells pealed magnificently from the new belfry and the whole neighbourhood took an enthusiastic part in the festivities.

After the Abbey Church was opened for worship in 1922 the priests of the community gave most of their time to the solemn celebration of the liturgy, the present Abbot told me, to which great care and attention was given. The Divine Office in the choir occupied some five hours a day of the monks' time. The lay brothers spent far less time in the choir and occupied themselves in the external work of the Abbey.

The 1930s saw an influx of young Englishmen to the community and the Abbot, Anscar Vonier, gave considerable thought to providing suitable work for the growing young community. This problem was not resolved until much later.

It was Anscar Vonier who appreciated that Buckfastleigh needed to have its own Roman Catholic Church and a site and a house were purchased in Chapel Street. The foundation stone of the new building was laid by the Bishop of Plymouth on the 11th July, 1939, and the first mass was celebrated by the parish priest on the 31st December, 1939.

When the Co-operative Wholesale Society took over the Woollen Mills in 1920 there had been a boom in the industry. However, soon after, a slump came and although the trade did pick up again it never really regained its former importance as a centre for the woollen industry. It wasn't only the woollen industry which went into a depression; in Devon as a whole the agricultural depression had hit hard; and, in Cornwall, several mines had been closed.

Many Devon workers migrated to other parts of the country in order to obtain employment with better rates of pay and more security. But to counteract this trend there came an influx of tourists which led to the development of Devon's major industry. Migrants came to the region in the form of temporary holiday visitors, elderly people wishing to retire and workers engaged in catering and personal service trades.

The four inland towns of the region, Newton Abbot, Totnes, Ashburton and Buckfastleigh, showed a similar trend of marked increase in pouplation during the 1920s, a movement which stopped and even reversed during the 1930s.

The change in the balance of power and of mobility which I mentioned earlier meant that more "ordinary" people could take advantage of the countryside and the facilities which it boasted, Dartmoor the coastal resorts and the fishing facilities; but for local people times still must have been as hard as always with a depression in industry and in agriculture.

"Ready to Serve!" Included in this group are Messrs. Coleman, Foot, Henley, Voden, Gomm, Roberts and Northcott about 1939. *Courtesy of Mr. E. Coleman.*

Chapter Twelve
THE SECOND WORLD WAR

The Second World War was for Buckfastleigh and Buckfast, as for the rest of the country, a period of marking time. As in the Great War an exodus of local men and women meant an additional burden for the women left behind to work in the woollen mill and on the land.

Buckfastleigh was subject to the same defence regulations as the rest of the country and Edgar Reed of Market Street, then a special constable, described certain incidents to me so fascinatingly that I repeat them here.

"The main roads around Buckfastleigh," Edgar told me, "were prepared with tank traps let into the road in concrete pits and able to be raised if an invasion came. At one stage in the war all the farmers in the locality were briefed to block all side roads with farm utensils and all sign posts were removed."

"The open moors were dotted with posts to stop the planes landing there. I often wonder," said Edgar, "whether local people knew that a concrete gun emplacement was in position at Bigadon, not far from the garage, so that fire might be directed at Torbay in the event of an invasion."

"Where Fairy Lane road leads down through the rocky hillside at Timbers and before it reaches the A38 there are two concrete slots one each side of the road in the walls. They were supposed to take a beam of wood to stop the tanks in an invasion!"

"Buckfastleigh's only experience of being bombed in the war came one Saturday afternoon on a fine day. I was standing talking to Reg. Laskey," said Edgar Reed, "on the top of Cock Hill, when we heard a plane coming in low. Then we heard the machine gun going and the school playground was hit. As the plane disappeared low over Church Hill what seemed like several small bottles dropped out of the plane and exploded in the field behind the mill. There were two large bombs, one which exploded near the church and the other which bounced down through the orchard above Buckfast Road, hit the road leaving a dent in it. It just missed two women out for a walk and crashed through the railings on the other side of the road, bounced into the field where the Caravan Park now is, jumped the river and finished up on the other side. The police put up a UXB danger notice and closed the road to Buckfast from Dart Bridge. This was in force for several hours until the bomb disposal squad arrived and found that there was no fuse in the bomb. It had been forced out of the bomb and was found eventually in the Car Park field. The bomb was then loaded into a lorry and carted away.

"The local population woke up one day," continued Edgar, "near the end of the war to find that the road to Totnes and all the side roads were closed from Dartbridge. People had to cycle miles around to get to their work.

"Armoured vehicles began to rumble into this road; there were three guards at Dartbridge, an American soldier, an English soldier and a civil policeman. Passes were issued to people living in this section to get to and fro. This operated as far as Shinners Bridge where a huge hole was dug and filled up with water. All vehicles were driven through this water.

"No American soldier inside this road was allowed to write home and it seemed obvious locally that the invasion of France was imminent," ended Edgar.

During this period Buckfastleigh and the surrounding district saw an invasion of a different kind. Although there was a considerable migration of women who married American servicemen and went to live in America, we welcomed a number of Polish men and women into the locality. At Holne Chase there was a Polish resettlement camp and several Poles were employed locally. Some married local people and their sons and daughters are Devonians with a different mixture of blood in their veins.

Chapter Thirteen
THE FURNEAUX FAMILY

THROUGHOUT this book the reader may have noticed references to the Furneaux family especially in the early chapters as, like many other notable families, it was more than probable that they came to England with William the Conqueror in 1066. Like the Hamlyns the Furneauxs have given a tremendous amount to Buckfastleigh and, also like the Hamlyns, have influenced its development.

The Rev. Tobias Furneaux writing from his family ntoes in 1845 states that the Buckfastleigh branch of the family descended from the Paignton branch, for the Furneaux were well known all over Devon, and can be traced back in Buckfastleigh to the seventeenth century. In fact, according to Tobias, they were probably one of the most important landowning families in the town (also involved in leather and wool) and records of their importance can be seen on tablets and tombs in the church, by the property they owned, and from the marriages they made with other well known important families.

It has proved a difficult task to fit together the family history, even from the history compiled by Tobias Furneaux, but one of the more well known members of the family was John Furneaux who became a director of the Hamlyn business in partnership with James Hamlyn in 1868. Like his partners and associates he was a keen business man active in public life especially in the church. In the centenary celebration booklet of the Wesleyan Sunday School (1811-1911) there is a fine picture of John Furneaux and, indeed, the booklet was written by the same John who described himself as a former teacher, secretary and Sunday School superintendent.

The booklet mentions other Furneaux such as Christopher Furneaux of Hapstead of whom he wrote, "Mr. Christopher Furneaux of Hapstead who used occasionally to assist by reading some interesting narrative and in giving out hymns." Apparently it was the same Christopher Furneaux who started the idea of a Sunday School treat by offering a bag of wheat — an extremely valuable commodity in those days.

John Furneaux is also mentioned in the Jubilee history book of the Co-operative Wholesale Society as being the first person to become a member, besides which he was a J.P. and chairman of the Totnes, Buckfastleigh and Ashburton Railway. It was John who built Harewood (formerly known as Hill Crest) where he lived for many years before eventually leaving Buckfastleigh to live in Clifton with a married daughter.

As there are over 300 baptisms of Furneaux recorded in Buckfastleigh up to the Second World War I do not feel guilty about not describing the whole family! But mention must be made of John Mudge Furneaux, described as a tanner, who, it was believed, was descended from Samuel of Button. He was also a prominent citizen who married Susan Bovey of Bilberryhill and built and lived in Oaklands for many years. He died in 1917. Various other members of the Furneaux family living at the time of the First World War were described as vaulable assets to the community and highly respected although they were not all landowners.

But what about now, some sixty-five years later? For there are still Furneaux living in Buckfastleigh today. The "Johns" of the Furneaux family still abound with John Furneaux marrying Joyce Balsdon in 1942. John and Joyce settled at Orchard Terrace in Buckfastleigh and had two daughters, Hilary and Margaret, both married, and one son, also called John, born in 1953.

John Dennis Furneaux married Melinda (Lyn) Wheeler in 1977 when he was twenty-four years old. Both John and Melinda live in Chapel Street and I am glad to say that there is little chance of the Furneaux family dying out as their first child is a son, Peter John and their second a daughter.

John and Lyn are typical of Buckfastleigh's young families today, happy to maintain their roots in the town and build a good family life. They are different from their landowning predecessors but nevertheless are important as the parents of the next generation of Buckfastleigh children and, important as people in their own right who, along with other local families shape the Buckfastleigh of the future.

John Furneaux about 1911.

John Furneaux (born 1953) with his son, Peter John (taken in 1981)

CONCLUSION

People without power or influence probably do not regard themselves as shapers of a town's future. However, the contribution of all local people affects the quality of life in a town or village as well as their own lives.

Alan Rogers in his book, *Approaches to Local History*, says, "All history and local history more obviously than many other branches of that study, concerns the inter-relation of people and place. The two have interacted on each other in a manner which is hard to disentangle." In the economic history of mankind, as much as in the topographical history of the settlement, the countless decisions of individuals have played a significant a part as the forces of geography."

So, Buckfastleigh, described in various ways such as "nestling in green hills . . . ." or "nestling in the valley of the Mardle or the Dart, well endowed with rivers, streams and farmland", has survived over 900 years of history. 900 years in which the town has produced inhabitants who have worked hard, not only for themselves, but that the town might benefit. Civil and other wars, religious uprisings, plagues and other diseases have all left their mark on the town, as they have in other places (and some events happened so long ago that there is no written record of them).

The population of Buckfastleigh has not fluctuated much over the past years. Before the Great War the population was 2,400. Today it is approximately 3,500. More housing is evident but there are smaller families living in them. I wonder how many of us feel the sense of history that pervades Buckfastleigh? I shall be satisfied if people feel that this book conveys even the merest sense of history of this town that we have inherited.

FORE STREET, BUCKFASTLEIGH 29008

PLYMOUTH ROAD, BUCKFASTLEIGH 29006

ACKNOWLEDGEMENTS

These are due to the following authors and publishers:

A. E. Andriette, *'Devon and Exeter in the Civil War'*, published by David & Charles Ltd.

Maurice Ashley, *'The English Civil War'*, published by Thames & Hudson Ltd.

Helen Harris, *'Industrial Archaeology of Dartmoor'*.

Penguin Books Ltd., publishers of Poetry by Robert Herrick, (introduced by John Hayward).

Alan Rogers, *'This was Their World'*, published by The British Broadcasting Corporation.

The House of Lords Record Library for giving me permission to reproduce the names of local inhabitants from *The Devon Protestation Returns for 1641*.

Dom John Stephan, *'Buckfast Abbey (A Guide and History)'*, published at Buckfast Abbey.

I would also like to acknowledge the help and support given by the following people:
The Abbot of St. Mary's, Buckfast Abbey, Mr. John Allen, Mr. E. J. Beer, The late Mr. Alfred Callard, Mrs. M. Callard, Mr. Arthur L. Clamp, Mr. and Mrs. Edward Coulton, Mr. and Mrs. John Furneaux (snr.), Mrs. J. Furneyhough (U.S.A.), The late Miss Joan Hamlyn, Mrs. Helen Harris, Mr. Edward Hunt, Mr. and Mrs. Stanley Harris, Miss Constance James, Mr. W. Joint, Mr. Leslie Lane, Mr. and Mrs. Michael Lane, Mr. Lodie, Mrs. G. O'Brien, Mr. Edgar Reed, Mr. J. W. Shinner, Mr. Gordon Stone, Miss Muriel Stone, Mr. J. Thompson, The late Rev. J. Timms, Mrs. A. Tonkin, Mrs. Edith Walters, Miss Marjorie Warren, The late Mrs. Willis.

BIBLIOGRAPHY

This was Their World, Approaches to Local History, Alan Rogers.
Victoria County History of Devon.
Centenary Celebrations Wesleyan Sunday School (1811-1911) Buckfastleigh, John Furneaux.
Jubilee History of Buckfastleigh Cooperative Society Ltd. (1869-1919), J. R. Dyer.
Buckfast Abbey, Dom John Stephan, (O.S.B., F.S.A., F.R.HIST.S.).
The History of the Furneaux Family.
Yesterday's Villages, Members of the Dartington Rural Archives.
Devon and Its People, W. G. Hoskins.
Kelly's 1910 and 1913 Directory.
Life in Tudor Times, Penry Williams.
Devon and Cornwall, A preliminary survey.
Fieldwork in Local History, W. G. Hoskins
White's 1850 Directory of Devon.
Industrial Archaeology of Dartmoor, Helen Harris.
The English Civil Wars, Maurice Ashley.
Dartmoor, A new study edited by Crispin Gill.
Devon and Exeter in the Civil War, E. A. Andriette.
The Cabells and Their Kin, Dr. William Cabell.
The History of the Hamlyn Family.

BUCKFASTLEIGH is a small manufacturing town on the river Dart and the high road from Plymouth to Exeter and London, having a station on the branch of the Great Western railway from Totnes to Ashburton, and is 22 miles south-west from Exeter, 6 north-west from Totnes, 21 by road and 30½ by rail from Plymouth and 195 by road from London and 230 by rail, in the Southern division of the county, Stanborough hundred, Stanborough and Coleridge petty sessional division, Totnes union and county court district, rural deanery and archdeaconry of Totnes and diocese of Exeter. The scenery around here, with Dartmoor in the distance, is very beautiful, and the trout and salmon fishing in the Dart is very good.

Under the provisions of the "Local Government Act, 1894" (56 and 57 Vict. c. 73), the original parish has been divided into East and West, the former governed by an Urban District Council of nine members formed December 4, 1894. The church of the Holy Trinity, standing on a lofty eminence, is an ancient edifice of stone in the Early English and Perpendicular styles, consisting of chancel, nave, aisles and transepts, south porch and an embattled western tower with spire containing 6 bells: there is a memorial window erected by Mr. and Mrs. John Fleming, of Bigadon, to their daughter, and two others to a former vicar and his wife, and to a Mr. James Powning and his son: the stained east window, with four smaller ones, were the gift of Richard John King esq. who formerly resided in the parish: the west window was erected by Miss Lowndes in memory of her parents: the carved oak pulpit is the work of the late Mr. John Pope: the covers of the Bible are also exquisitely carved: in 1897 the chancel was renovated and redloored, and a new altar presented, the cost being defrayed by John Fleming esq. J.P. of Bigadon, and his wife: there are 400 sittings. East of the church, but detached from it, is an ivy-clad ruin, possibly the remains of an old chantry chapel. The parish register dates from the year 1602. The living is a vicarage, net yearly value £205, with 14½ acres of glebe, and residence, in the gift of R. A. B. Fleming esq. and held since 1908 by the Rev. Henry Frank Nesbitt M.A. of Clare College, Cambridge. St. Luke's chapel of ease, in Plymouth road, was erected in 1894 on a site presented many years ago by the late J. Maye esq. of Barkington, and was dedicated by the Bishop of Exeter, October 22nd in the same year; the cost, amounting to about £1,800, was defrayed by subscriptions, £500 being given by Mr. J. Symons. The great tithes, arising out of the lands comprised within the manor of Brook and the town manor, belong mostly to the Earl of Macclesfield, and those arising out of the lands within the manor of Kilbury to Jeffery Edwards esq. and the rector for the time being of the sinecure rectory of Ermington in this county, now the Rev. Edmund Pinwill M.A. of Pembroke College, Oxford; the last mentioned great tithes formed part of the possessions of the monastery of Montague, in the county of Somerset, on its dissolution. There is a Wesleyan chapel in Chapel street and a smaller one at Buckfast; and a Congregational chapel, first founded in 1787; the present edifice was built in 1872, at a cost of about £1,350, and has 400 seats. Buckfastleigh Town Hall and Institute in Bossell road, erected on freehold ground at a cost of £1,350, is a building of local limestone, with Bath stone and brick facings, and comprises a spacious hall, 6rft. by 31ft. with a stage for various purposes measuring 23ft. by 14ft.; the hall will seat 450 persons: there is also a library, billiard room, with a large table, the gift of H. B. Mildmay esq., and club and reading rooms, with a residence for the caretaker: the whole is managed by a committee of 5 members. The woollen manufacture is carried on here and large contracts are executed for the supply of navy serge, coating tweeds and blankets. There are also a woolcombing factory, a paper mill, an iron foundry and two tanneries in the town; in the neighbourhood are lime and limestone quarries, and tin and copper mines, but at the present the two last named are not worked. Black Rock and Bakers pits, near the parish church, have several openings leading into a series of caverns which extend for considerable distances. The fairs formerly held here on the third Thursday in June and the second Thursday in September have been discontinued. There are several charities, the principal being one in the hands of the feoffees for the maintenance of the fabric of the parish church; Mrs. White's of £500 invested in Consols is for 16 widowers and 16 widows; there are also several minor charities producing about £14 yearly, which sum is distributed by the vicar and churchwardens. The abbey of Buckfastre or Buckfast is said by common local tradition to be more ancient by some centuries than the neighbouring town of Buckfastleigh; which, in fact, was originally the "ley" or pasturage belonging to the abbey: the Saxon name was "Buckfæsten," i.e. "deer-fastness," as appears from Bishop Aelfwold's charter, granted about 1035: the Saxon abbey of S. Mary of Buckfæsten was probably founded in the reign of King Cynewulf, c. 760, and about 1110 passed to the Grey Monks of Savigny, and in 1138 to the Cistercians; at the period of its surrender by the last abbot, Gabriel Donne, there were 10 monks, and revenues estimated at £465: after the Dissolution the roofs of the abbey buildings were stripped of their lead, and for nearly two centuries the ruins appear to have furnished building materials for the locality: the site remained uninhabited till 1796, when the erection of a house in the Gothic style on the west side of the destroyed cloisters was begun, and finished in 1806: the abbey, situated 1 mile north of the village on the right bank of the river Dart, included a fine church, 210 feet long internally, and consisting of choir with aisles and eastern chapels, transepts 85 feet north to south, also with eastern chapels, nave with aisles, and probably a central tower; on the south side were cloisters, 100 feet square, with sacristy adjoining the south transept, next, the chapter house, 40 feet by 20 feet, slype and fratry, or common room, and then the frater (refectory) and kitchen; and on the west side the "cellarium;" at the south-west angle of the cloister was a Perpendicular tower with stair turret, still in good preservation, and the tithe barn, a large structure 100 feet in length, is also extant, but of the church, and other buildings, only scattered fragments, some archways and other entrances and portions of the foundations are left. In 1882 the abbey was purchased from Dr. Gale, of Plymouth, by a colony of Benedictine monks from Pierrequi-vire in Burgundy, who with the aid of a committee presided over by Lord Clifford Chudleigh resolved gradually to rebuild the abbey. On February 24, Feast of St. Matthias, 1903, Dom Boniface Natter O.S.B. was solemnly blessed and installed as the first abbot of the restored succession by the Right Rev. Bishop Graham of Plymouth. In 1906 the newly elected abbot was lost in a shipwreck and the Right Rev. A. Vonier O.S.B. a survivor of the same wreck, was elected in his place: under his direction the rebuilding of the monastic church on its old foundations was at once commenced: at present (1910) the whole of the eastern portion and two bays of the nave are up to the height of the aisle window heads; dark grey local limestone is being used for the outside of the building, and Bath stone for the inside: the whole of the work is being carried out by the lay brethren themselves under the direction of Frederick A. Walters esq. F.S.A. architect, of Westminster. The chief landowners are the Earl of Macclesfield, who is lord of the manor, the trustees of the late John Fleming esq. of Bigadon, Mr. William R. Coulton, quarry owner, J. Bickford esq. and Messrs. Hamlyn Brothers. The soil is loamy; subsoil, slate and limestone; the chief crops being wheat, barley, pasture and apples. A large quantity of cider is made, most of which is of very superior quality. The area of East Buckfastleigh and Urban Council District is 1,355 acres of land and 11 of water; rateable value, £9,828; population in 1901, 2,520; and of Holy Trinity ecclesiastical parish, 2,781.

The area of West Buckfastleigh is 4,509 acres of land and 7 of water; rateable value, £2,461; the population in 1901 was 261.

Sexton, James Chaffe.

Post, M. O. & T. Office (letters should have Devon added).—Wm. Chaffe, postmaster. Letters delivered at 7 & 11.5 a.m. & 4.45 p.m.; sundays, 7 a.m.; dispatched at 9.10 & 10.35 a.m. & 2.40 & 6.45 p.m.; sundays, 2 p.m

Buckfast Post Office.—Miss Violet Baker, sub-postmistress. Letters received via Buckfastleigh are delivered at 7.20 & 11.30 a.m. & 5.20 p.m.; dispatched at 8.10 a.m. & 12 noon & 6 p.m.; sundays, 7.20 a.m. Buckfastleigh, 1 mile distant, is the nearest money order & telegraph office

Wall Letter Boxes.—Market street, cleared at 8.30 a.m. & 2.20 & 6.25 p.m.; sundays, 8.30 a.m.; Runnaford Combe, at 9.25 a.m. week days only; Bossell, at 7.50 a.m. & 2.25 & 6 p.m.; sundays, 7.50 a.m.; Springfield, at 9.15 & 11.15 a.m. & 4.50 p.m.; Dart Bridge, at 8.20 a.m. & 12.10 & 5 p.m.; sundays, 8.20 a.m.

URBAN DISTRICT COUNCIL.

Meets at the Club room, Town hall, 2nd monday in the month at 5.45 p.m.

Members.

All retire in April, 1915.

Chairman, William Hamlyn.
Vice-Chairman, John Willcocks

James F. Bowerman
William Bradford
William Allen Brooks
Edward James Coulton
Joseph Hamlyn
Cooper Mitchell
William Northcott

Officers.

Clerk, Edward Windeatt, solicitor, Totnes
Treasurer, Wm. Fredk. Telfer, Lloyds Bank Lim Totnes
Medical Officer of Health, Henry Ubsell M.R.C.S.Eng. Hill crest
Surveyor & Sanitary Inspector, Andrew Warren, Rock cottage
Collector, Andrew Warren, Rock cottage

PUBLIC ESTABLISHMENTS.

Town Hall & Institute, W. H. Furneaux, hon. sec.; F. W. Bennett, caretaker
Volunteer Fire Brigade, Fore street, W. H. C. Pugsley, captain, & 10 men
Police Station, John Sprague, constable

PUBLIC OFFICERS.

Assessor & Collector of King's Taxes, James Roger Petherbridge, Fore street
Assistant Overseer for East Buckfastleigh, Andrew Warren, Rock cottage
Assistant Overseer & Clerk to the Parish Council for West Buckfastleigh, William Lyddon Bennett, 9 Bossell terrace
Certifying Factory Surgeon for Buckfastleigh & Brent, Henry Ubsdell M.R.C.S.Eng. Hill crest
Medical Officers & Public Vaccinators, Totnes Union, Buckfastleigh District, George Michie M.A., M.B., C.M.; Staverton & Battery Districts, Henry Ubsdell M.R.C.S.Eng. Hill crest
Registrar of Births & Deaths, Buckfastleigh Sub-district, Totnes Union, John Bovey, jun
Deputy Registrar of Births & Deaths, John William Warren, Fore street
Registrar of Marriages, Jas. Roger Petherbridge, Totnes Union, Fore street
Town Crier, James Chaffe, Fore street
Vaccination Officer for Buckfastleigh & Ugborough Districts of Totnes Union, John Bovey, jun

Buckfastleigh directory of 1910. This detailed account of the area shows the extent of the town before the changes which came after the 1914–18 conflict. The community in 1910 was probably at its most independent state being very self sufficient and varied. The two wars, the use of the car and greater mobility of the people were to change this record of a South Devon town. See back cover for remaining information.

PUBLIC ELEMENTARY SCHOOLS.

A School Committee of nine managers was formed in September, 1903; G. Windeatt, Totnes, correspondent to the managers; Frank Loveridge, St. Lawrence la. Ashburton, attendance officer

Buckfastleigh, with master's residence, were erected in 1875, at a cost of £2,959; they contain separate rooms for boys, girls & infants, with class rooms attached to each; average attendance, boys, 130; girls, 130 & infants, 130; Alfred George Abbott, master; Miss Mary Greenfield, mistress; Mrs. Elizabeth Butler, infants' mistress

Buckfast (mixed), erected in 1894, for 145 children; average attendance, 26; Miss Florence Lee, mistress

Coombe, erected in 1886, for 100 children; average attendance, 45; Miss Elsie Cole, mistress

Roman Catholic, Buckfast, erected in 1893, for 160 children; average attendance, 56; Sisters of Charity, mistresses

---

Railway Station, Thomas Edward Hewitt, station mastr
Great Western Railway Co. Harry Blackford, agent, Fore street

PLACES OF WORSHIP, with times of services

Holy Trinity Church, Rev. Henry Frank Nesbitt M.A. vicar; sundays, 11 a.m.; also sunday in the Buckfast Institute at 3.30 p.m

St. Luke's chapel of ease, sundays 8 a.m. & 5.30 p.m.; week days at 8 a.m.; also every fourth sunday at Scoriton at 3 p.m

Immaculate Heart of Mary (Cath.); priests of the Abbey officiate; sun. & holidays of obligation, mass, 6.30, 7, 8.30 & 10 a.m.; vespers, 3 p.m.; rosary, sermon & benediction, 6.30 p.m

Congregational, Rev. John Whale; 11 a.m. & 6.30 p.m. & thurs. 7.30 p.m

Wesleyan Methodist, 11 a.m. & 6.30 p.m.; mon. & thurs. 7.30 p.m.
Wesleyan Methodist, Buckfast (South Devon Mission); 3 & 6 p.m.; tues. 7.30 p.m.
} Rev. Ernest A. Stead

BUCKFASTLEIGH.

Residents at Buckfast Abbey.

Vonier Eight Rev. Anscar (abbot) O.S.B
Edmond Very Rev. Boussard (prior) O.S.B
Hauler Rev. Mellitus (parish priest) O.S.B
Rechtsteiner Rev. Winfrid (procurator) O.S.B
Brüchlen Rev. Martin O.S.B
Buguet Rev. Joseph O.S.B
Dillenz Rev. Richard O.S.B
Graf Rev. Ernest O.S.B
Keniry Rev. F. Augustine O.S.B
Louismet Rev. Savinian O.S.B
Massé Rev. Maurus O.S.B
Schneider Rev. Wilfrid O.S.B
Stephan Rev. John O.S.B
Weller Rev. Arnold O.S.B

PRIVATE RESIDENTS.

Barrington Mrs. Winsley, Buckfast
Betts Miss. Lourdes
Bunclark Mrs. Chapel street
Churchward Robert Edred, Hill side
Cornish William Henry, Black rock
Floyd Mrs. Sideham, Buckfast
Fleming Mrs. Bigadon
Furneaux John J.P. Tor view
Furneaux William, Rose cot. Silver st
Hall Miss, Bulberry hill
Hamlyn Joseph, Fullaford
Hendy Isaac, Steps house
Hoare Charles, Rockville
Ireland Mrs. Cleavehurst
Knowles Mrs. Liesse, Buckfast
Mason John, Springfield house
Michie George M.A
Mitchell Cooper, Plymouth road
Nesbitt Rev. Hy. Frank M.A Vicarage
Patteson Misses, Barnsfield
Rendell William, Buckfast
Smith Cyril A. Crippin's park
Stead Rev. Ernest A. (Wesleyan)
Strickland Misses, St. Joseph's
Trelawny John Salisbury, Harewood
Ubsdell Hy. Marldon ho. Hill crest
Waller Mrs. Oaklands
Warren Andrew, Rock cottage
Whale Rev. John (Congregational)
Willcocks John, Moorfield
Willcocks Miss. Fore street
Williams Sydney Rice M.B. Toll Marsh
Wilson Mrs. Bossell

COMMERCIAL.

Early closing day, Tuesday 2 p.m.
Arscott & Son, builders, Plymouth rd
Barnicoat Richard, baker, Market st
Barrett Charles, butcher, Fore street
Bennett Frederick William, caretaker of the Town hall
Bennett William Lyddon, assistant overseer & clerk to the parish council for West Buckfastleigh, 9 Bossell terrace
Berry John & Sons Limited, serge manufacturers, Buckfast mills
Bickford John, solicitor (attends fridays), Fore street
Blackford Harry, omnibus proprietor, Fore street
Bovey John, jun. registrar of births & deaths for Buckfastleigh subdistrict & vaccination officer for Buckfastleigh & Ugborough districts of Totnes union, & insur. agt
Bowerman Jas. Fergus, Mechanics' Arms
Bradford Wm. grocer & draper, Fore st
Buckfast Gas Works (F. Hawkyard, proprietor)
Buckfastleigh Co-operative Society Limited, Chapel street
Butchers & Co. grocers, Market st
Butchers Alfred J. china & glass dealer, Plymouth road
Callard & Son, coal & corn merchants
Cann John, confectioner, Chapel st
Capital & Counties Bank Lim. (The) (sub-branch of Ashburton); open tues. & fri. 11.15 to 1.45 o'clock, Fore street; draw on head office, 39 Threadneedle st. London EC
Chaffe James, town crier & bill poster
Chaffe Wm. woollen draper, "Real Devonshire Serge" depôt, suitings & ladies' dress serges; also tweeds. Weech serge warehouse
Churchward John & Sons Limited, seed merchants & woollen manufacturers, Fore street & woollen manufacturers, Harbertonford
Churchward Gilbert, carpenter, Fore st
Coode Albert Edward, tailor, Fore st
Coode Philip, Fore street
Coulton W. R. & Sons, stone quarry owners
Cousins Alexander, chemist, Fore st
Craig Frank Sydney, farmer
Cricket Club (H. J. French, sec.), Tor view
Cussley Saml. boot ma. Plymouth rd
Daw Louis, White Hart P.H. Plymouth road
Devon & Exeter Savings Bank (W. Bradford, agent), Fore street
East Ann W. (Miss), grocer, Market
Fire Brigade (Volunteer) (W. H. C. Pugsley, captain), Fore street
Football Club (Richd. P. Tarring, sec)
Foster George, Globe P.H. Chapel st
Furneaux Samuel & Son, builders, Plymouth road
George Silas W. watch ma. Fore street
Gidley John, thatcher, Silver street
Gillard Samuel, boot & shoe maker, Fore street
Gillard Thomas Hall, painter, Fore st
Hamlyn Bros. Ltd. woollen manufrs
Harvey Frank, dairyman, Higher town
Heywood Eli, shopkeeper, Market st
Hoare Elizh. (Mrs.), butcher, Fore st
Hoare William, wheelwright, carpenter & english timber merchant, Plymouth road
Honywill Thomas, Royal Oak P.H. Jordan street
Horswill Charles, farmer, Bigadon frm
Horticultural Society (Gilbert Churchward, sec.), Fore street
Hosking Bros. furn. dlrs. Plymouth
Hunt Charles, painter, Fore street
Hunt Charles (Mrs.), milliner, Fore st
Hunt Lewis, baker, Fore street
Hurd Albert, insur. agent, Chapel st
Jackson & Son, builders, Jordan st
Lane Maria (Mrs.), shopkpr. Fore st
Lewis Annie (Miss), frmr. Abbey farm
Lidstone Jas. hair dresser, Chapel st
Lloyds Bank Limited (sub-branch of Totnes) (open tues. & fri. 11 a.m. to 2.30 p.m.); draw on head office, 71 Lombard street, London EC
Luckraft Thomas, ironmonger, Fore st
Maidwell Fanny (Mrs.), King's Arms hotel, Fore street
Masonic Lodge (The Trinity) (No. 2595)
Memory Thomas, insurance agent
Michie George M.A., M.B., C.M. physician & surgeon, medical officer & public vaccinator for Buckfastleigh district, Totnes union
Millman & Sons, undertakers, Plymouth road
Moore George, photographer, Fore st
Peachey Abraham Edward, wheelwright, Dart bridge
Pearce Walter James, farmer
Pengelly Edwd. boot ma. Chapel st
Penny Edward, watch maker, Fore st
Penny Wilfred E. boot maker, Fore st
Perriton John, apartments, Kilbury
Petherbridge James Roger & Son, ironmongers, Fore street
Petherbridge E. (Mrs.), milliner, Plymouth road
Petherbridge James Roger, collector of King's taxes, & registrar of marriages, Totnes union, Fore st
Petherbridge Jn. insur. agt. Coxhill
Pinkcombe Fredk. tailor, Jordan st
Pugsley Wm. Jas. insur. agt. Fore st
Reed John & Son, grocers, Market st
Reed & Smith, paper makers, Dart ml
Rew Henry, farmer, Brambleby
Rice Jas. Furneaux, baker, Fore st
Rogers Wm. Hy. butcher, Market st
Roper Frederick, shopkeeper, Fore st
Scott John, farmer, Grange, Buckfast
Searle Elizh. A. (Miss), stationer, Fore st
Seaward Wm. boot maker, Market st
Setters John, Bridge inn
Shaw William John, fruiterer & greengrocer, Fore street
Shute Edwin, baker, Fore street
Smith Elizabeth Ann (Miss), fancy repository, Chapel street
Stancombe Jacob, Half Moon P.H. Plymouth road
Stone Eliza (Mrs.), aparts Rockfield
Symons John & Co. Limited, cider makers & merchants; & at Totnes
Tolchard Mary Ann (Mrs.), Golden Lion P.H. Chapel street
Tolchard Victor, hair dresser, Fore st
Town Hall & Institute (W. H. Furneaux, hon. sec.), Bossell road
Trist Geo. (Mrs.), milliner, Market st
Ubsdell & Williams, surgeons
Ubsdell Henry M.R.C.S. Eng. (firm, Ubsdell & Williams), surgeon, & medical officer & public vaccinator, Staverton district, Totnes union, & certifying factory surgeon for Buckfastleigh, Ashburton & Brent, & medical officer of health to the Urban District Council
Wakeham Samuel, dairyman, Chapel st
Wall Gordon Stuart, fancy dlr. Fore st
Warren Andrew, surveyor, sanitary inspector & collector to the Urban District Council, assistant overseer & architect, Rock cottage
Warren John Chaffe, farmer, Rill frm
Warren John William, saddler, & deputy registrar of births & deaths, Fore street
Weeks John, carpenter, Chapel street
Weeks Walter, Sun inn, Market street
White Celia (Mrs.), Town Arms P.H. Market street
White Frank, Valiant Soldier P.H. Fore street
Willcocks & Son, engineers
Williams Sydney Rice M.B. Lond., M.R.C.S. Eng., L.R.C.P. Lond. (firm, Ubsdell & Williams), physician & surgeon, Toll Marsh
Wotton Edwd. Thos. painter, Fore st
Wright Herbert Edward, Waterman's Arms P.H. Higher town
Young Men's Christian Association (William Bradford & E. Jones, secs.), Chapel street

BUCKFASTLEIGH WEST.

Hamlyn William, Hapstead
Heath John, Scoriton
Tanner Edmund Fearnley J.P. Hawson court

COMMERCIAL.

Abbott John (Mrs.), farmr. Wallaford
Barter John, farmer, Warnacombe
Beard Henry, farmer, Button
Beard Jn. Herbt. farmer, Northwood
Chamberlain Robert, farmer, Runnaford Coombe
Codd William, butcher & farmer
Commons Tom, farmer, Forder
Coombes James, cowkeeper, Coombe Barton
Heath John, farmer, Scoriton
May Arth. W. frmr. Runnaford Coombe
Petherbridge James Roger, farmer, Green Down
Rew Henry Sydney, farmer
Rowland John, farmer, New parks
Rowland Wm. Jn. frmr. Hawson frm
Sampson Edwin H. farmer
Sampson Henry H. farmer, Bowerden
Stephens Philips, farmer
Symons Arthur, Tradesman's Arms P.H. Scoriton
Turner Charles, farmer, Scoriton
Wills Robert Northcott (Mrs.), farmer, Bowden
Wilton Henry, farmer
Wilton John, farmer, Hapstead farm

Continuation of the Buckfastleigh directory of 191 showing the private residents and commercial interest of the town.

Arthur L. Clamp – the man behind the books

Arthur Leslie Clamp was a man of boundless energy with a passion for helping others, particularly through his love of history. A printer by trade, he started his career in a printing company before moving his family from Exeter to Plymouth to teach at the Plymouth College of Art and Design, where he eventually became the Head of the Printing Department.

Arthur with his five children.

A Devoted Family Man

Despite his love of teaching, Arthur prioritised his family, always making it home by 5:30pm for tea. He and his wife, Rosemary, raised five children: Susan, Angela, Elizabeth, David, and Steven. Arthur would often combine his love of family and history by taking his children on Sunday walks, encouraging them to appreciate historical monuments by taking photos or making crayon rubbings of gravestones for his books. The family home at 203 Elburton Road was a hub of activity, with a large garden, featuring a two-storey fort and a makeshift swimming pool.

A Lifelong Learner and Adventurer

Arthur's thirst for knowledge extended beyond history to a deep curiosity about the world. He was passionate about exploring different cultures, traditions, and cuisines, often taking advantage of his long summer holidays as a teacher to travel to places like India, Russia, South America, the middle east and the USA, sometimes bringing one of his children along. This adventurous spirit even influenced his home life, as seen by the short-lived family tradition of steam-cooking vegetables after a trip to Iceland.

History is a prominent feature of family days out

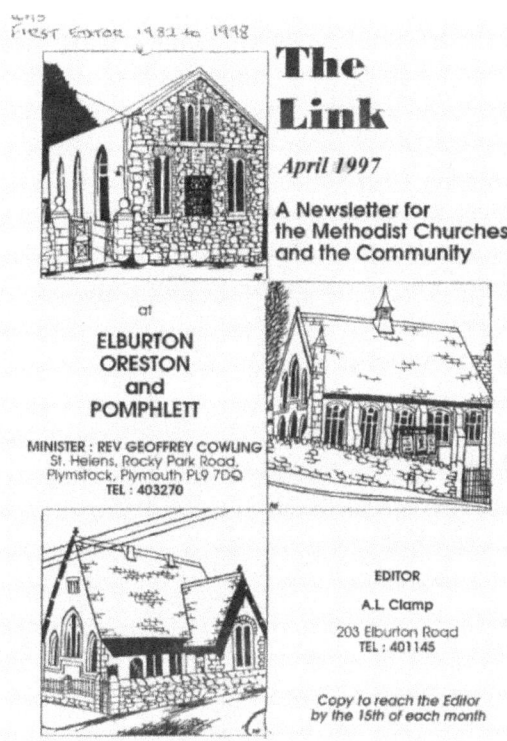

Community and Philanthropic Spirit

His commitment to serving others was evident in his long-standing involvement with the Elburton Methodist Church. He was the Sunday School Superintendent for over 15 years and served as the editor of the wider church's monthly newsletter, "The Link," for a similar duration. After Rosemary's very sad passing, Arthur later remarried and, following a chance encounter with a professor from India, established a connection with a missionary school in Chennai. Together with his new wife, Christine, he co-founded a "Sponsor a Child's Education" program that continues to this day.

*Pictured left – The cover of 'The Link' complete
with hand drawn sketches of each church by Angela
Below right – Arthur Clamp promoting his latest book
Below left – Arthur at home with his first wife, Rosemary
Below centre – Arthur on holiday with his second wife, Christine*

A Legacy of Learning and Positivity

Arthur's greatest passion was history, which he brought to life through tireless research, documentation, and the many books he authored. He was driven by a need to "never be stuck in a rut," constantly seeking new experiences, meeting new people, and expanding his knowledge. With a positive attitude and a great sense of humour, he was always ready to help others, leaving a lasting impact on his family and community. His children, Susan, Angela, Elizabeth, David, and Steven, remember him with love and gratitude.

David Clamp, 2025

A Legacy of Local History

Below is the story of how Arthur L Clamp began writing books, in his own words, drafted shortly before he passed away in 2001. I have only made minor alterations to this text, correcting grammatical errors that he did not survive to correct himself. When I first discovered this text, I was shocked to see my name mentioned. It seems that, unbeknownst to me, I shared my first PC with him. I suspect he used it during the day when I was at school, although I do have one memory of sitting with him and showing him how it worked. It has been a pleasure to pick up where he left off and see his books republished and redistributed, and to know that I was part of the story, even back then. It was also fascinating to discover that his pricing structure matches the way I have tried to price the books, with a third going to local sellers and the rest covering printing costs with a little left over for my expenses.

I am his eldest grandson, and it is a privilege to curate his legacy, which we are calling 'The Clamp Collection'. The very last line of the text originally reads "The following pages list all the titles." Sadly, that page is missing and we have no record of all the books he published and knowing that some of those were researched by other authors makes the process of finding them even harder. I look forward to one day completing the collection and seeing them all available again. And maybe, one day, I'll even start writing my own to add to the series. For now, here is his story in his own words.

Steven Gibson, 2025

Writing and Publishing Booklets on Local Topics and Areas

I started this interest in either 1968 or 1969 when living in Woodford. I had by these dates established the Department of Printing and I think I must have been looking for something different to do. The first titles were of A5 size proofed from type set at Clarke, Doble and Brendon, Ltd., Plymouth printers, and then made up into pages and printed at Sawtell and Neilson, Ltd., Totnes.

Then began a slow process of getting them out to shops, etc. which proved to be more time consuming and difficult than actually researching, writing and getting the books into print. However, I persisted and opened a business account with Barclays Bank on the Broadway. I was advised to give it a title so I called it "Westway Publications". There came along another problem, one of storage of paper and finished books which was solved when the family moved to Elburton in 1970.

I changed the printer to Penwell, Ltd., Callington, Cornwall, as he was then just setting up himself and his prices seemed very reasonable. I did not get any of the printers to make up the complete books. I hand folded the flat printed sheets, stitched the books on a small manual table stitcher and trimmed them in a small hand turned guillotine which I bought from someone in Penzance for £40. It was brought up in a van.

The trouble and time going to and fro to Callington was too much so I transferred the printing to PDS Printers, Prince Rock, Plymouth, and I have been with them ever since. Now they are at Plympton which is easy to reach and they fold the flat sheets which was turning out to be a long chore which only saved a small part of the printing costs.

All my first titles were written by myself. I took the photographs and developed them in the loft of the house, the type was set by now on a computer situated in the house at Elburton from which I had collected photographic lengths of text to cut up and law down as pages.

At some point I decided that I would do my own film processing of lith film so I bought a large second hand process camera from Kingsbridge and learnt through trial and error to make line negatives of the text and halftone negatives of the illustrations which proved more difficult than I anticipated. The main problem was trying to keep the developer in the large dish at the correct temperature as any change would affect the developing time. I replaced this old camera with a brand new one bought from Croydon, Surrey, costing £900. This has turned out to be a great asset cutting out an expensive part of the printer's costs and one crucial aspect of the work which I could control.

By the middle 1970s there were many outlets I had contacted in Plymouth, up to Dartmoor, Exeter, around to Torbay, Totnes, Dartmouth and the South Hams. The market for local books was much greater than I had first thought and through getting to know many local people undertaking research themselves had the chance to help and make up books for other people who had in most instances, got together a collection of photographs with some text in a rather muddled way. Through my experience in print I was able to shape up their work and get it into print and in every case I had to pay the printer and let the person have the royalties. In the majority of titles produced in this manner this was another way of producing titles and it did give some profit to my work. However, I must say that in a few cases I lost out by either the other person getting the numbers wrong, not returning any monies from stock I delivered or they thought that more of their books should have been sold.

The print run was usually 1,000 copies and from time to time I have had reprints of 250 copies. It took about ten years to clear the first print run so I always had large stocks in the garage, workshop, etc. The numbers sold during the early years was about 7,000 copies a year increasing to around 9,000 copies and for the whole of the enterprise about 500,000 have been sold. The booklets have become part of the local scene and many people collect them, shops regularly order copies and I go around certain areas month by month restocking or replacing titles as necessary.

During the past year or so I have started setting the text on a Packard Bell PC, something which I should have done some years back. I share it with Steven Gibson, my grandson. There appears to be no end to the market for local books, but I could not earn a regular income because of the long time it takes to sell stock.

However, now exceeding 100 titles made up mainly of A4 twenty-four page booklets, some folded guides, with selling prices set with a third going to the shop which is the trade custom, the original idea has been quite successful and could go on for ever.

Apart from monetary benefits, however spasmodically these might be, I have learnt a lot myself, met many interesting people and have become part of the local scene with requests to give talks and to advise people about getting into print.

Arthur L Clamp, 2001

This newspaper article, published by the Evening Herald on 17th August 2001, forms a good record of his life. Just as he encourages us to learn more about local history, we encourage you to learn a little about him. For that reason, we have included these pages at the back of all the most recently republished books, in honour of his memory and recognition of his contribution to the community.

www.ingramcontent.com/pod-product-compliance
Lightning Source LLC
Chambersburg PA
CBHW061403070526
44584CB00031B/4153